TEACHING THE ACTUALITY OF REVOLUTION

AESTHETICS, UNLEARNING, AND THE SENSATIONS OF STRUGGLE

TEACHING THE ACTUALITY OF REVOLUTION

AESTHETICS, UNLEARNING, AND THE SENSATIONS OF STRUGGLE

Derek R. Ford

Published by *Iskra Books* 2023

Iskra Books
Madison, Wisconsin
U.S. | U.K. | Canada | Australia | India
Iskra Books is an independent scholarly publisher—publishing
original works of revolutionary theory, history, ecology, and art, as
well as edited collections, new translations, and critical republications
of older works.

ISBN-13: 978-1-0880-7169-4

British Library Cataloguing in Publication Data
A catalogue record for this book is available from the British Library

Library of Congress Cataloguing-in-Publication Data
A catalog record for this book is available from the Library of
Congress

Cover Art: *El Mapa* by Daniela Chaparro
Cover Design and Typesetting by Ben Stahnke
Printed and Distributed by IngramSpark

CONTENTS

"In our eventful time, just as in the 16ᵗʰ century, pure theorists on social affairs are found only on the side of reaction and for this reason they are not even theorists in the full sense of the word, but simply apologists of reaction."

—*Friedrich Engels*
Preface to the Third Volume of Capital

INTRODUCTION

THE CONJUNCTURE OF POLITICS, AESTHETICS, AND EDUCATION

B arely an hour goes by, it seems, without another piece from the public intellectuals of the educational "global theory in-dustry." Lacking any roots in the existing people's struggles of the day, this industry's educational "activist-scholars" provide a radical cover for anti-communist and anti-revolutionary pol-itics. Despite their constantly expanding list of neoliberalism's ills and vague endorsements of unexamined social movements, they ultimately wage the class struggle in the academy on behalf of imperialism. Recent historical research by Gabriel Rockhill explains why these intellectual commodities circulate so widely: they're in line with the ruling classes' project to "redefine the Left—in the words of cold warrior CIA agent Thomas Bra-den—as the 'compatible,' meaning non-communist, Left."[1] In the educational arm of this industry, an abundance of ambigu-

---

1   Gabriel Rockhill, "The CIA & the Frankfurt School's An-ti-Communism," *The Philosophical Salon*, 27 June 2022.

ous rhetoric camouflages the absence of any political alternatives and deflects from any precise inquiry into the role of education in reinforcing or resisting any political order. Critiques are in themselves pedagogical or education is positioned as in need of critique and transformation.[2]

Teaching the Actuality of Revolution not only presupposes the revolutionary project, but it follows a different path for pedagogical politics. In this opening cleared by Tyson E. Lewis, educational "politics does not begin with changing a student's beliefs or raising critical consciousnesses" and instead "has its fleshy roots in the pre-reflective, pre-cognitive erotics of perceptual foreplay wherein the potentiality for sensing differently—sensing otherwise than the disciplinary apparatus of learning dictates—is not sacrificed but rather nurtured."[3] Although educational politics for me *is* about beliefs and ideas, it's *also* about perceptions and sensations and, just as importantly, the interplay between the two. No sensations are pure, immediate, or uninformed by what we think or believe, and the politics of any pedagogical form encased in concrete historical moments either reinforces the existing order of things or challenges them by opening up other possibilities. This provides an initial link between educational politics and aesthetics, as education necessarily reinforces, rearranges, and/or challenges dominant regimes of perception, ways of seeing, feeling, smelling, hearing, and tasting.

---

2   See Derek R. Ford, *Politics and Pedagogy in the "Post-Truth" Era: Insurgent Philosophy and Praxis* (London: Bloomsbury, 2019), 3-5.

3   Tyson E. Lewis, "Studied Perception and a Phenomenology of Bodily Gesturality," in C. Mayo (ed.), *Philosophy of Education 2013* (Urbana: Philosophy of Education Society, 2013), 346, 347.

Just think of how much of our elementary school experience is explicitly about enforcing a particular regime of the senses: "Don't lick *that*!" "Sit down and *listen to me*!" "Stop looking *out the window* and bring your eyes to the board!" It's the same with teachers in that we can *see* certain students as intelligent or stupid, as good or bad investments, as members of racial, gender, and other social groups—or not. Educational aesthetics is partisan in that it "produces a practical mode of intelligibility of political processes, which is fully incorporated into subjects' apprehension of themselves and the world."[4] Capitalist education—and maybe all education–unavoidably produces the fit or misfit between ourselves and the world by teaching how we can and can't, or how we should or shouldn't, see, hear, touch, smell, and taste.

A critical analysis of capitalism and the struggle for socialism, then, must attend to the aesthetic dimensions of both. Capitalism isn't a purely economic system; it is a perceptual apparatus. Capital is a perceptual ecological system, a dynamic and interactive network producing forms of "common sense," and just as capital is historically produced through struggle, so too are our perceptual capacities, orientations, and regimes. "The sensuous world," Marx and Engels write in *The German Ideology*, "is, not a thing given direct from all eternity, remaining ever the same, but the product of industry and of the state of society; and, indeed, in the sense that it is an historical product, the result of the activity of a whole succession of generations [...]

---

4   Jennifer Ponce de León, *Another Aesthetics is Possible: Arts of Rebellion in the Fourth World War* (Durham: Duke University Press, 2021), 248.

modifying its social system according to the changed needs."[5] In this section of the manuscript, written between 1845-1846 but unpublished until 1932, they're critiquing one of the Young Hegelians they're breaking with, Ludwig Feuerbach. For Feuerbach, we achieve liberation by directly sensing the world as it is, by achieving "sensuous certainty." Marx and Engels reject the possibility of sensuous certainty because even the most basic object of our senses results from "social development, industry, and commercial intercourse." Giving the cherry tree as an example of a "simple" and "common" sensuous object, they observe that the tree was "only a few centuries ago transplanted by *commerce* into our zone, and therefore only *by* this action of a definite society in a definite age it has become 'sensuous certainty.'"[6]

Comparing this formulation with Marx's unpublished manuscripts from 1844 reveals the great leap—or dare I say break—they made in this short timespan. Marx's 1844 work upholds Feuerbach's belief that "sense-perception in the twofold form both of *sensuous* consciousness and *sensuous* need" constitutes "*true* science."[7] Endorsing the sensuous certainty he'd shortly repudiate with Engels, Marx admits that the production of the senses comprises "the entire history of the world down to the present" while simultaneously arguing that each sense has its own specific and natural "*essential power*." We read Marx wrestling through the contradictions to formulate a materialist ap-

---

5   Karl Marx and Friedrich Engels, *The German Ideology: Part One*, trans. C.J. Arthur (New York: International Publishers, 1932/1970), 62.

6   Ibid.

7   Karl Marx, *Economic and Philosophic Manuscripts of 1844*, trans. M. Milligan (Mineola: Dover Publications, Inc., 1961/2007), 111.

proach even as he affirms the separation of the senses and attributes "the peculiarity of each essential power" of distinct senses to "its *peculiar essence*," such that "to the *eye* an object comes to be other than it is to the *ear*."[8]

In *The German Ideology*, Marx and Engels clear new ground for the historical materialist or, as they phrase it, "the *practical* materialist, i.e. the *communist*."[9] "Communists in practice," they state, "treat the conditions created up to now by production and intercourse as inorganic conditions, without, however, imagining that it was the plan or the destiny of previous generations to give them material."[10] The distance Marx and Engels established in the course of a few years enables them to propose that our sensuous capacities, their organization, and the entire sensuous world are historically produced. They even suggest that "so much is this activity, this unceasing sensuous labour and creation the basis of the whole sensuous world as it now exists, that, were it interrupted only for a year, Feuerbach would not only find an enormous change in the natural world, but would very soon find that the whole world of men and his own perceptive faculty, nay his own existence, were missing."[11] There's no predetermined or unchanging relationship between any sensuous object and faculty.

Sound, for example, interacts with our bodies through vibrations. We *feel* the vibrations of a booming base while riding in a car and *see* the vibrations of the musicians playing on a stage. The idea that listening is the essential property of the

---

8   Ibid., 108.

9   Marx and Engels, *The German Ideology*, 62.

10   Ibid., 86.

11   Ibid., 63.

ear wouldn't make sense before the widespread availability and affordability of the phonograph, the first accessible technology that separated music from the spatial, temporal, and social context of its performance. The inability to see performers "was once a source of great anxiety," as Mark Katz documents, and when first hearing music on record players "listeners simply stared at their phonographs."[12] Katz references a 1923 *Journal of Educational Method* article where educational theorist Stephen G. Rich writes that his experience using record players in schools "convinced me that the machine should be turned *with its back to the audience*" and positioned in the corner of classrooms. "The usual procedure of having the machine face the audience," Rich proposes, "is only an unthinking inheritance from the days when we had no phonographs, and when we naturally had to look at the performer."[13] The shape and structure of our sensations and that which we sense are determined by the different modes of production operative in the past, present, and future of any social formation.

My argument is that capital's perceptual ecology is—and must be—continually reinforced through educational processes. Because the sensuous world is produced by "the total living sensuous *activity* of the individuals composing it," it can be transformed by "the communist materialist" who "sees the necessity, and at the same time the condition, of a transformation both of industry and of the social structure."[14] If this production rests on

---

12   Mark Katz, *Capturing Sound: How Technology has Changed Music* (Berkeley: University of California Press, 2010), 22, 24,

13   Stephen G. Rich, "Some Unnoticed Aspects of the School Use of Phonographs," *Journal of Educational Method* 3, no. 1 (1923): 111.

14   Marx and Engels, *The German Ideology*, 64.

a specific educational modality, then we communist materialists ought to develop alternative aesthetic and pedagogical frameworks to produce them differently. Entering the class struggle aesthetically is important at this moment because, despite the endless proliferation of ever-more refined critiques of it, the reproduction of capital continues.

Explication and critique are crucial, but they don't define the entirety of the class struggle, and even they take aesthetic forms that configure the sensual world. Interestingly, Marx's famous claim in *The Eighteenth Brumaire of Louis Bonaparte* that we produce history not as we want to but "under circumstances directly encountered, given and transmitted from the past" is a claim about the aesthetics of political language. "Social revolution," he continues, "cannot draw its poetry from the past, but only from the future."[15] The aesthetic representation of working and oppressed peoples is part and parcel of the class struggle and is not limited to any particular arena of production. Anything can take on what Jan Mukařovský calls the "aesthetic function," and no discrete boundaries separate "the aesthetic and the extra-aesthetic."[16] The aesthetic function "is not a real property of an object" and only appears in definite "conditions."[17] The class struggle produces these definite conditions as well as our current sensual experiences and competencies and the theories we use to understand and transform both. Because our dominant sensual

15   Karl Marx, *The Eighteenth Brumaire of Louis Bonaparte*, trans. C.P. Dutt (New York: International Publishers, 1852/1963), 15, 18.

16   Jan Mukařovský, *Aesthetic Function, Norm and Value as Social Facts*, trans. M.E. Suino (Ann Arbor: University of Michigan Press, 1970), 1.

17   Ibid., 28, 3.

organization is reproduced *pedagogically*, resistance requires alternative pedagogical dynamics that become political through the course of struggle.

RETHINKING PEDAGOGY AND POLITICS IN CLASS STRUGGLE

Whenever political organizers and researchers focus on the pedagogical *theories* in our work, the most customary and easily identifiable starting point is critical pedagogy, a field that is often incorrectly associated with Paulo Freire, given that Freire never categorized his work under that heading. Moreover, as Curry Malott proves in his reading of founding texts in the field by the likes of Henry Giroux, Stanley Aronowitz, and Donaldo Macedo, "the history of what is known as critical pedagogy began in the 1980s as a conscious break from Marxist educational theory and capitalism's communist horizon."[18] There are, to be sure, notable exceptions in the realm of educational theory, many of which center around what Paula Allman termed "revolutionary critical pedagogy."[19]

Peter McLaren, a student and comrade of Freire's, articulates revolutionary critical pedagogy to transition the broader field of critical pedagogy "into the service of altering historical modes of production and reproduction in specific social formations, including if not especially educational formations."[20] Focusing on education's role in the reproduction of labor-power, Glenn Ri-

---

18   Curry S. Malott, "In Defense of Communism: Against Critical Pedagogy, Capitalism, and Trump," *Critical Education* 8, no. 1 (2017): 5.

19   Paula Allman, *Critical Education Against Global Capitalism: Karl Marx and Revolutionary Education* (Rotterdam: Sense, 2010).

20   Peter McLaren, "Revolutionary Critical Pedagogy," *Interactions* 6, no. 2 (2010): 5.

kowski thinks of ways to produce educational crises to interrupt that process (thereby creating crises for capital), and Dave Hill's policy proposals lay the groundwork for such crises.[21] Wayne Au emphasizes the more molar ways pedagogy is politicized, writing that "pedagogy can provide the *how* we teach to change the world," but it isn't "just what we do in schools or classrooms. Every day, we teach ourselves and each other, learn from ourselves and each other, and make decisions about how we approach all of our relations."[22] Sandy Grande's Red pedagogy, for another example, engages revolutionary critical pedagogy's "vision as one of many starting points for rethinking Indigenous praxis."[23]

Collectively, McLaren, Rikowski, Hill, Au, Grande, and others practice education "as a form of activism and community organizing" to transform not only modes of production but ways of thinking and being in the world on singular and collective levels.[24] This body of praxis (of which I've relayed just a fraction) truly traverses the boundaries between schooling and society. At the same time, the definitions of and relations between education and social transformation are underarticulated at the level of theory. If teaching *is* politics or a kind of activism,

21 Glenn Rikowski, "Crisis," in S. Themelis (ed.), *Critical Reflections on the Language of Education: Dangerous Words and Discourses of Possibility* (New York: Routledge, 2021); Dave Hill, "Classical Marxism, Ideology and Education Policy," *Critical Education* 13, no. 1 (2022): 70-82.

22 Wayne Au, *A Marxist Education: Learning to Change the World* (Chicago: Haymarket Books, 2018), 194.

23 Sandy Grande, *Red Pedagogy: Native American Social and Political Thought*, 10th anniversary ed. (Lanham: Rowman & Littlefield, 2004/2015), 32.

24 Au, *A Marxist Education*, 151.

what particular kind is it? What specifically and generally distinguishes pedagogy from politics?

There's a tension between pedagogy and politics, at least as I see and define them in our current era. Politics is the struggle for power that combines direction, ideological content, and organizational and mass struggle. Pedagogy names the *forms* and *relations* of education. Pedagogy takes diverse and even contradictory forms, so it isn't determined entirely by a political platform. Politics, by contrast, is binary as it's a struggle for the power to realize a definite partisan program. At the same time, my wager is that pedagogy can contribute to political struggles by offering educational forms organizers can utilize at various levels *with* the appropriate and correct content. In other words, I'm not saying that we should isolate education's *form* from its *content*, let alone elevate the former over the latter. Both the *what* and *how* of education are politically decisive, but my interest in this book is primarily in pedagogical form. That said, the same pedagogical form can either reinforce or challenge capitalism depending on its deployment in a particular conjuncture.

The conjuncture is a concrete analysis of a particular situation. Yet this isn't a simple investigation into the events, situations, or characteristics of a moment or era. In the conjunctural analysis, the various elements of the situation "become real or potential forces in the struggle for the historical objective, and their relations become relations of force."[25] What makes the conjuncture unique is that it encompasses the existing factors—whether they be political groupings and ideologies, social conditions or modes of production, state or global actors—relative to

25   Louis Althusser, *Machiavelli and Us*, trans. F. Matheron (New York: Verso, 2000), 19.

the revolutionary project. This approach works within a marxist framework to identify the pedagogical, political, tactical, and strategic elements, whether they be manifest or latent, existing or possible, to achieve the actuality of revolution, and the conjuncture as it's determined by the objective of revolution determines the relations between aesthetics, education, and politics at any given moment. Yet there is also something pedagogical about the conjunctural analysis itself. Marxist theory is predicated on the unexpected twists and turns of the movement and develops as the class struggle reflects on itself, a reflection, in turn, that depends on our pedagogical tactics and educational philosophies.

The class struggle's terrain encompasses the production and reproduction of our perceptions, aesthetic relations, sensual world, and the knowledge that produces and is produced by each. In our conjuncture, after decades of near unrestrained U.S. imperialism, Jennifer Ponce de León astutely observes that the possibility of other worlds is "*aesthetically* rendered invisible, impossible, or forever deferred."[26] Oppositional struggles should engage with the existing but repressed possibilities that permeate our global struggle, for which pedagogy offers a hinge. Although pedagogy is pivotal in marxist history and, as the first chapter establishes, in Marx's own work, it's generally underexamined. My intention is neither to provide a formula for the "correct" marxist pedagogy or the "real" or "true" pedagogical relationship between aesthetics and politics, nor is it to tell organizers what to do or how to teach. Instead, I want to contribute to the collective development of common theories, concepts, and practices for revolutionaries in the U.S. to use as we plan,

26   Ponce de León, *Another Aesthetics is Possible*, 8.

practice, reflect on, and refine (or redefine) the pedagogical dimensions of the movement overall, including its organizations,
activities, publications, and formal education.

We can't create oppositional pedagogies without first ap-
preciating the educational apparatus we're up against today in
formal education and society overall, which is characterized, as
the second chapter argues, by the pedagogy of learning. Think of
how we're always encouraged to learn, to be "lifelong learners,"
and how so many fundamental social issues—from unemploy-
ment to mass incarceration—are posited as problems we can
solve through learning.[27] The reduction of education to learning
is a significant victory for our class enemies. For one, it eclipses
the need for *teaching* and *teachers* in that one can learn without
a teacher's expertise or authority to determine *what* the student
should learn or otherwise engage. Teachers are no longer experts
but service providers there to meet the needs of learners and, as
my university president told incoming first-year students, faculty, and staff during our 2022 opening convocation "employers,"
effectively transforming education into a market exchange. For
two, learning describes a *process* (one can learn anything) whereas education describes a process with an *orientation* and *direction*. Now that learning has become naturalized and valorized
in itself, what one learns is ultimately dictated by the need to
remain competitive in the hyper-malleable global market.

In response to the domination of education by learning,
Gert Biesta characterizes teaching as "something that comes

---

27   See Derek R. Ford, *Marxism, Pedagogy, and the General Intellect: Beyond the Knowledge Economy* (New York: Palgrave Macmillan,
2021).

radically from the outside."[28] When learning from a teacher, the student brings the teacher's knowledge into their existing outlook and way of being. When being taught by a teacher, the student's life is interrupted as the teacher intervenes in the being of students through arranging educational material, generating relationships of trust, and cultivating spaces for unexpected encounters. When I think back to those who have taught me, their lessons have always been ones I couldn't have anticipated or even known I needed at the time. In most cases, they were difficult and even painful lessons.

Biesta argues—and I agree—that education is *defined* by the act of teaching because "the point of teaching, and of education more broadly, is never that students 'just' learn, but always that they learn *something*, that they learn it for particular *reasons*, and that they learn it *from someone*."[29] Despite the fact that teaching is, by definition, oriented around certain desired objectives, it is not guided by the production of something new (an act, body, mindset, disposition, etc.) per se. Education is responsible for providing students the opportunity to study and respond to the teacher's knowledge uniquely and without predetermined outcomes. For education to be liberatory, however, it can't be straightjacketed by a predetermined trajectory, nor can it be idealistically posited as completely open, because without a political framework openness reinforces the current order.

The liberatory teacher, then, who teaches for the actuality of revolution, is decidedly *not* "a 'guide on the side' or backstage

---

28   Gert J.J. Biesta, *The Beautiful Risk of Education* (Boulder: Paradigm Publishers, 2014), 46.

29   Gert J.J. Biesta, *The Rediscovery of Teaching* (New York: Routledge, 2017), 27-28.

'facilitator' who moves forever sideways, slipping out of his or her responsibility to actively direct the pedagogical process." As McLaren maintains, the teacher is rather "cobra-like, moving back and forth and striking quickly when the students' conditioning was broken down enough so that alternative views could be presented."[30] Some are frustrated by "the assertive generality of Freire's formulations of and pronouncements on pedagogy," but McLaren correctly sees it as a strength that's consistent with "his refusal to spell out in a 'bag of tricks' fashion alternative solutions."[31] Marxism is a living, breathing doctrine, a guide to action above all else, there are no permanent and transcendental knowledges, strategies, or tactics. As it is in politics, so too is it in pedagogy.

Political teaching requires producing something different altogether, an alternative aesthetic and political reception of and relation to the world; the possibility of a political subject to carry out the revolutionary task. Yet political teaching as I'm thinking of it in this book is not political because it closes the gap between this world and another (which would collapse pedagogy into politics), but because it organizes an educational experience of the gap itself. Rather than "make sense" of something according to the current order of sensibility, the teacher prompts another kind of sense-making by challenging the sensual regime of capital and promoting a new collective imaginary. The imaginary is, in Rockhill's words, "a collectively produced practical mode of intelligibility that assembles self-evident givens, being at one and the same time a way of thinking, feeling, being, per-

---

30   Peter McLaren, *Che Guevara, Paulo Freire, and the Pedagogy of Revolution* (Lanham: Rowman & Littlefield, 2000), 151.

31   Ibid., 164.

ceiving, and acting."[32] Creating a new collective imaginary is a political project while, for me, cultivating the encounter with another set of possibilities within the present is a pedagogical project. Taylor R. Genovese is right to insist that our moment "necessitates that we must cultivate within ourselves both the fighter and the aesthete."[33] Yet the link between these two requires the production of the pedagogue, as well.

By educating ourselves and others about education, we increase our power to act in organizational and movement settings to produce a new revolutionary imaginary. This book works through some political, aesthetic, and pedagogical dynamics to amplify and refine this revolutionary imaginary by experimenting with some potential educational theories for the revolutionary struggle. Above all, the aim is to stimulate a sense of possibility and wonder amongst the collective that might pick it up over time. While wonder on its own remains ahistorical and abstract, linking wonder with possibility orients theory toward particular objectives. This is a pressing need since, as Jodi Dean frames it, today we believe that "there are revolutions, but they are not for us, not the revolutions we were hoping for, not proletarian revolutions."[34] Rejuvenating and popularizing our belief in the actuality of revolution is a primary objective of organizing.

---

32 Gabriel Rockhill, "Temporal Economies and the Prison of the Present: From the Crisis of the Now to Liberation Time," *Diacritics* 47, no. 1 (2019): 18.

33 Taylor R. Genovese, "Translator's Introduction," in Alexander Bogdanov, *Art and the Working Class*, trans. T.R. Genovese (Madison: Iskra Books, 2022), 21.

34 Jodi Dean, "The Actuality of Revolution," in J. Cutter (ed.), *Storming the Gates: How the Russian Revolution Changed the World* (San Francisco: Liberation Media, 2017), 134.

To insist on the actuality of revolution is not to declare that revolution is guaranteed or inevitable; it is not an empirical assertion but a basic theoretical principle central to marxism. Always unpredictable, there's nothing to guarantee where or when the revolutionary rupture will take place, that revolutionary forces can—and will—seize the opportunity, that reactionary forces won't seize the moment of insurrection, or that existing forces won't quickly reabsorb the opening back into the capitalist mode of production. The party neither knows if or when the revolutionary moment will come, nor can it call the revolution into being. The party does operate on the assumption of, in Georg Lukács' distillation, *"the fact—the actuality—of the revolution."*[35] The actuality of revolution is a perspective dictating our actions today, guiding our every move in the here and now, as the party is "consistent and flexible in adhering stubbornly to its principles and simultaneously holding itself open to each new daily development."[36]

Teaching the actuality of revolution transforms our *sense* and *understanding* of struggle's possibility. In this way, it provokes unlearning the current capitalist construction of time, marked as it is by the ubiquity of the *now*, or when "individual moments are uprooted, fragmented, and disconnected." This creates a "fixation on the now, or what we might call *urgentism*" that "obfuscates our historical conjuncture, meaning the ways in which the present is rooted in the past and structurally intertwined with a very specific future."[37] The urgentism of the now

---

35   Georg Lukács, *Lenin: A Study on the Unity of His Thought*, trans. N. Jacobs (New York: Verso, 1924/2009), 26.

36   Ibid., 36.

37   Rockhill, "Temporal Economies and the Prison of the Present,"

is prominent in the academy, where the only dogma we can't question is that "the delusions and superstitions of yesteryear," with their promise of rebellion and a new mode of production, "no longer have any purchase."[38] It's hard to imagine a radically different future when the demands of the now confine our thinking.

Marx's work makes such an imagination possible, as one of his main findings is that time isn't linear, chronological, stageist, universal, or developmental. History isn't a *thing* but an imprecise metaphor that, if used incorrectly, flattens time. Marx rejects Hegel and critiques Proudhon, for instance, for their teleological conception of philosophy and history. His introduction to his *Grundrisse* notebooks exposes how "the so-called historical presentation of development is founded, as a rule, on the fact that the latest form regards the previous ones as steps leading up to itself," a rule only overcome if historical presentation is "able to criticize itself."[39] Capital, as we'll see in the next chapter, *tries* to produce a sense of time that is teleological, continuous, and uniform. In response, marxist pedagogy can help others know and experience the diverse senses of time and modes of production in any social formation, connecting our current conjuncture with the ongoing developments of the class struggle and the imagination of revolution's actuality.

22.

38 Gabriel Rockhill, *Radical History and the Politics of Art* (New York: Columbia University Press, 2014), 92.

39 Karl Marx, *Grundrisse: Foundations of the Critique of Political Economy (Rough Draft)*, trans. M. Nicolaus (New York: Penguin Books, 1939/1973), 106.

The Conjuncture of the Educational Intervention

There's no binary between theory and practice in marxism. It's not as if marxism is something you "apply" or "use" to analyze a situation. Even the term "praxis" is ambiguous in this regard, for theory *is* a form of practice, although one that is clearly distinct from others. Still, just as "*there is no concrete analysis of the concrete situation without minimal mastery of Marxist theory*," neither is there marxist theory or pedagogy without a concrete analysis of the concrete situation.[40] As a generalized reflection on the class struggle in concrete times and places, marxist theory and practice begin with an analysis of the conjuncture. Marxist theory is a materialist intervention in the class struggle in a concrete context and situation for definite political goals.

Under what conjuncture do the aesthetic and pedagogical theories offered in the following pages intervene? One that's unique and daunting. As communist organizer and theorist Brian Becker notes, "the greatest danger to a revolutionary process is not the experience of a political downturn, such as we have experienced during the past decades."[41] In the history of the international workers' movement, setbacks are more common than advances. Our conjuncture is unprecedented and overwhelming. It's greater than a defeat: it is "that the theory of revolutionary Marxism and the entire vision of workers' power has been discredited and isolated from the people's struggles."[42] Histor-

---

40   Louis Althusser, *What is to be Done?*, trans. G.M. Goshgarian (Cambridge: Polity Press, 2018/2020), 11.

41   Brian Becker, "Praxis: Revolutionary Theory and Practice in the Present," in D.R. Ford (ed.), *Keywords in Radical Philosophy and Education: Common Concepts for Contemporary Movements* (Boston: Brill, 2019), 339.

42   Ibid., 340.

ically, practical political activity retracted after such defeats—although marxist theory persisted and, in fact, even advanced, as revolutionaries deepened inquiry to revive the struggle. After the overthrow and dissolution of the Soviet Union and the Eastern Bloc socialist states, marxism was wiped from and discredited in the people's movements.

Defeats of previous revolutionary movements were always the product of *struggle*. The Soviet Union's overthrow was so catastrophic, however, as a result of "the character and form of the defeat." While mobilizations occurred, there were "no long-lasting barricades, no prolonged fighting in the streets" as, in general, "confusion, passivity and inertness were widespread."[43] Because the breakup of the Soviet Union happened without any real struggle (as forces inside the state dismantled it), this tragic setback didn't stimulate a new wave of revolutionary praxis but profoundly fractured the continuity of marxism. "The organizational lessons from previous generations of struggle," as Becker points out, "have been suppressed. If some people have criticized the idealism of the 1960s and 1970s generation—for prematurely believing that revolution was imminent—today's problem is the opposite and far more challenging: the assumption that socialist revolution will never happen, and the masses will always be oppressed."[44]

In the U.S., and much of the world, the working class and oppressed have increased our practical political activity, al-

---

43   Brian Becker, "Introduction: The Importance of the 100th Anniversary of the Russian Revolution," in J. Cutter (ed.), *Storming the Gates: How the Russian Revolution Changed the World* (San Francisco: Liberation Media, 2017), xiv, xv.

44   Becker, "Praxis," 341.

though marxist theory is no longer the guiding thread of our movements. Most obviously with the Bernie Sanders phenomena, socialism—but not quite marxist *theory*—is once again becoming ascendant. The practical, political, and ideological conjuncture is shifting in ways favorable to overcoming the interruption in the ideological continuity of our movements. Upticks in spontaneous struggles are becoming more and more common, creating educational *opportunities* for more and more people in the *sensations of struggle*, the *feeling* of revolutionary possibility, and the *knowledge* of revolutionary theory. The tasks before us are in large part, then, aesthetic and pedagogical.

MAPPING THE BOOK

Much intellectual work on marxism (and education) focuses on demystifying the "false" appearances by unveiling their "true" reality. The first chapter surmounts the limits of these projects by demonstrating how capital is an aesthetic ecological regime that's about cognition and sensation, or knowledge and aesthetics. Our class struggle needs to cultivate an aesthetic encounter with alternative lifeworlds in the present and to enunciate the educational resources involved as we contend with the aesthetics of our reasoning and criticism, such as the perceptual effect of our writing. The first chapter maps the aesthetics of capital and the class struggle to claim that Marx's method and aesthetic pedagogy correspond to—and work against—the forces of capital. Drawing a constellation of the perceptual ecology of contemporary capitalism, I delineate how capital shapes our sensuous capacities and tendencies. Turning to the relations between art, politics, and pedagogy, I argue that through our collective work and action in the world we learn and relearn the right modes of perceiving and knowing the world, ourselves, and each other. I pick up on a latent—sometimes explicit but still underdeveloped—pedagogical project in recent scholarship on marxism and aesthetics that encompasses collective mapping and the production of sensations of possibility. I then address how the political objectives of Marx's *Capital* are taught through a particular form of aesthetic pedagogy, focusing in particular on the fetishism of commodities and *so-called* primitive accumulation.

Having outlined the broader setting, the second chapter takes up the function of pedagogy in the reproduction of capital. I address *teaching* and connect the reigning praxis of teaching as the facilitation of learning to the maintenance of capital's rule, showing how we're schooled to sense the world through the lenses of commodity exchange, individuality, and optimization, all of which limit our collective imaginary, channel our outrage into appropriate channels, and keep us fragmented and divided. In response, I advance teaching as the organization of unlearning through moments of breakdown, which makes the familiar strange, disidentifies us with capitalist ideology, and pushes us into new perceptual apparatuses.

As the second chapter discusses the different educational processes of learning and unlearning, the third chapter explores the different methods of thinking involved in both. I focus on Louis Althusser's analysis of certain artists and artworks to analyze his thinking on aesthetics and politics. Althusser positions art as that which produces the sensorial experience of knowledge in the making, or the immersion in the disjuncture of thought through which we experience a revolutionary alternative in the present moment. My engagement with Althusser goes against the grain of the standard and widespread interpretations of his theory and pedagogy. While Althusser says little about it, his pedagogical practices and theories have been widely critiqued from various angles.[45] The most infamous one comes from his former student, Jacques Rancière, who denounced Althusser's pedagogical practice as one where the teacher's role "is to transmit knowledge to those who do not possess it," a principle "founded only on the technical division of labor" between the student and professor.[46] Althusser represents the epitome of a "philosopher king" who begins by assuming an inequality between the teacher and student, repressing the latter's equality by imparting his knowledge to gradually bring the student closer to Althusser's level without ever eliminating the inequality between the two. As I draw out in this chapter and the next, the lesson I learn from Althusser is different: it teaches me to sense and think about a radical equality by moving pedagogy and politics from the cognitive to the aesthetic, by moving from the ahistorical temporality of capitalism to the Historical moment of revolution.

The fourth chapter moves to sound and the matter of listening and silence. I start with a pedagogical problem Althusser identifies in his short unpublished text, *What is to be Done?* where he suggests that the insufficiency of the workers' struggle in Europe at the time resulted from its failure to conceptualize the totality of the class antagonisms. He introduces but abandons the necessity to teach the ability to listen adequately.

---

45   For a history of these (mis)readings in education, see David I. Backer, "History of the Reproduction-Resistance Dichotomy in Critical Education: The Line of Critique against Louis Althusser, 1974-1985," *Critical Education* 12, no. 6 (2021): 1-21.

46   Jacques Rancière, *Althusser's Lesson*, trans. E. Battista (New York: Continuum, 1974/2011), 144.

Correct listening, interestingly, includes the ability to listen for what neither we nor our fellow class members know. We sense the radical indeterminacy of Althusser's theory and pedagogy as they ask us to listen for a silence beyond cognition. Theoretically, I develop a model of symptomatic listening and distinguish hearing from listening to help flesh out the kind of sonic relation he's after.

It would be a political and theoretical error to conclude from the above that decentering the subject and embracing contingency are universally revolutionary in themselves precisely because capital operates as an ecological network. The fifth chapter explains that uncertainty and unpredictability are sources of accumulation for capital in our current conjuncture. Turning to one of Althusser's contemporaries, against whom he's often pitted, I analyze Henri Lefebvre's project of attuning our class to the rhythms of everyday life in place of capital's domination over the times and spaces of our world. Lefebvre says capitalism is reproduced partially through the tyranny of abstract rhythms over concrete rhythms—the tick of the clock versus the movements of people and the Earth. Contemporary U.S. capitalism, however, achieved Lefebvre's project by finding sources of accumulation in the shifting and flexible rhythms of everyday life. Post-Fordism appropriates the opening of unforeseen and uncalculated new desires, events, and knowledges by placing them under the demand for production and actualization so that real revolutionary breaks seem impossible. Building on Jason Wozniak's work, I position arrhythmia—the break in rhythms—as an initiation into the actuality of revolution.

The conclusion returns to a pedagogical project that comes at the end of Rockhill's book on art and politics: the mapping of the conjuncture in which art and politics emerge. Fredric Jameson's pedagogy of "cognitive mapping" enters here as an aesthetic and political endeavor to teach a different aesthetic through the production of maps that relay different sensorial regimes beyond our visceral and cognitive amplitudes. Cognitive mapping involves charting out our location within the totality of capital, learning about contradictions, and through that very effort, unlearning the perceptual order of capital. We experience our inability to know the world as cognitive mapping is an impossible task. Taking up Fred Moten's critique of Jameson's misreading of the historical Black liberation struggle, I address Jameson's emphasis on and isolation of sight and the eye, proposing a perceptual mapping that reorders the senses so we can feel the ongoing struggle over their historical production and unlearn capital's perceptual ecology. While brief, I hope that the conclusion can place some of the necessarily abstract concepts in the book back into the context of totality and make them more accessible through what serves as both a concrete practice and a general model.

I end here with an important reminder: the socialist project *has*, through organized and coordinated efforts, produced aesthetic regimes where use-value got the upper hand over exchange-value, determining the rhythms of life and creating collective, common subjects. This process occurred throughout all arenas of life and the social, from international relations built on solidarity to cooperative economic planning guided by people's needs rather than profits, from urban planning and housing construction to dynamic musical cultures where workers from different nationalities and races became collective artists and blurred the lines between intellectual and physical labor, between amateur and professional.[47] I do this to not only reaffirm the actuality of revolution but to locate contemporary organizing within the long and complicated history of the marxist movement. But if you don't make it that far, at least remember this: Exploitation and oppression are not natural or permanent but social and transitory. Revolutions are not only possible but actual, not only a future aspiration but an undisputable accomplishment. We still don't know what our class is capable of inventing and unleashing.

This is not only a political point but a pedagogical one. How can we—and why would we—engage in the struggle if we didn't believe in the ability of our people to take power and reorganize society, if we didn't presume our collective competence? This educational philosophy that anchors this book can be traced back in the marxist movement to the founding of the International where, as Marx and Engels recall, "we expressly formulated the battle cry: The emancipation of the working class must be achieved by the working class itself [...] Hence, we cannot co-operate with men who say openly that the workers are too uneducated to emancipate themselves."[48] A (if not *the*) central

47   See Noah Leininger, "Music, not Muddle: Re-Examining Soviet Sounds and the Socialist Project," *Liberation School*, 08 September 2020. Available here: liberationschool.org/re-examining-soviet-music-and-socialism; Michal Murawski, "Actually-Existing Success: Economics, Aesthetics, and the Specificity of (Still-)Socialist Urbanism," *Comparative Studies in Society and History* 60, no. 4 (2018): 907-937; and Albert Szymanski, *Is the Red Flag Flying? The Political Economy of the Soviet Union* (London: Zed Books, 1979).

48   Karl Marx and Fredrich Engels, "Marx and Engels to August Bebel, Wilhelm Liebknecht, Wilhelm Bracke and Others (Circular Letter)," trans. P. Ross and B. Ross, in J.S. Allen, P.S. Foner, D.J. Struik, and W.W. Weinstone (eds.), *Marx and Engels Collected Works (Vol. 45): Letters*

ingredient in forging a vehicle for the working and oppressed to take power has always been the genuine belief in the people to take history into their own hands, which in itself validates that educational theory is foundational for the class struggle.

CHAPTER 1

PEDAGOGY AND THE PERCEPTUAL ECOLOGY OF CAPITAL

An ideology is effective to the extent that it's unquestioned, taken as natural, and assumed as timeless rather than the result of ongoing struggles over the production of perception. There's nothing more ideological than presenting something as non-ideological. Ideology isn't an error in—and corrected through—thought. Moreover, thought doesn't only take place in an entity called "the mind" that is autonomous from "the body," where the former thinks and the latter senses. Any critique or transformation of capitalist ideology, then, must engage the cognitive and sensual atmosphere that naturalizes, dehistoricizes, and depoliticizes our world. This opening chapter shows how Marx's *Capital* performs just this kind of ideological analysis, establishing, among other things, that Marx's *critique* of political economy is not about detailing the "truth" that lies behind the "false," but representing the contradictions of capital as a perceptual ecology. While Marx *describes* this ecology he also *demonstrates* it through a performative aesthetic pedagogy that produces a sensorial void in the reader. The elements of this pedagogy are determined by the *object* of study and Marx's political *objectives*.

I start with an introduction to the aesthetics of capital. Beginning with the fetishism of commodities, I briefly survey the three volumes of *Capital* to articulate a perceptual ecology of capital's logic by looking at the various forms and realities it produces. The next section highlights how art and politics (and the relationship between the two) are historically produced through various struggles, which clarifies the relationship between aesthetics, pedagogy, and politics. Identifying a latent but underdeveloped pedagogical project in research on the aesthetics of class struggle allows me to advance the formulation of pedagogy as a sociohistorical nexus between political economy and aesthetics; in other words, the pedagogy of *Capital* operates to explain, intervene in, and affect capital's overall perceptual ecology.

The aesthetics and pedagogy of political struggle are historically contingent on given social formations, assemblages of different modes of production, distribution, and consumption, and different modes of sensation. The last section argues that Marx's aesthetic pedagogy of presentation emanates from the object of study to leverage capital's contradictions, the contingencies of history, and the unknowability of the future to teach the actuality of revolution. I first examine Marx's critique of *so-called* primitive accumulation to disprove readings that relegate it to a past, accomplished, and universal narrative and, by doing so, provide what I argue is a more accurate understanding of Marx's analysis and indicate how his incongruous and conflicting presentation of capital's origins allow us to sense the possibility of revolutionary society here and now. I then return to the fetishism of commodities, which was first introduced in the 1872 German and 1872-75 French editions of *Capital* for what I interpret as pedagogical purposes.

THE AESTHETICS OF CAPITALIST IDEOLOGY

Ponce de León and Rockhill introduce the "compositional model of ideology" to describe "the intricate ways in which 'social agents' are gradually composed—and potentially recomposed—out of palimpsestic processes of material socialization."[1] Our subjectivity, consciousness, and sensuousness are the product of both the overall complex determinations of history and everyday encounters that either reinscribe, alter, or challenge our ways of making sense of the world. Ideology in this model is viewed as "a social process of habitual sense-making that norms perception, thought, and practice—among other things—by accustoming social agents to a shared sensorium."[2] At one point in their argument, they turn to Marx's writing on commodity fetishism from the first volume of *Capital* to demonstrate how this social process operates on both a macro and micro level.

Commodity fetishism names the reality under capitalism where "the social character of men's labour appears to them as an objective character stamped upon the product of that labour, because the relation of the producers [...] is presented to them as a social relation, existing not between themselves, but between

---

1   Jennifer Ponce de León and Gabriel Rockhill, "Towards a Compositional Model of Ideology: Materialism, Aesthetics, and Cultural Revolution," *Philosophy Today* 64, no. 1 (2020): 106.

2   Ibid., 101.

the products of their labour."[3] Commodity fetishism explains why when I purchase groceries I think and feel like an individual exchanging one object (money) for other objects, when I'm actually a social subject in a complex interaction with the international working class and the totality of capital. When I buy strawberries, I'm engaging in "a complicated affair involving dozens or hundreds or thousands of people, complex politics concerning tariffs and taxation (and maybe even the enforcement of these policies), contradictory border policies and innumerable decisions by banks, fertilizer companies, labor contractors, and much, much more."[4]

Ponce de León and Rockhill underline how Marx frames commodity fetishism as aesthetic. As Marx writes, commodities are "social things whose qualities are at the same time perceptible and imperceptible by the senses," just like how "the light from an object is perceived by us not as the subjective excitation of our optic nerve, but as the objective form of something outside the eye itself." The difference is that as values, commodities have "absolutely no connexion with their physical properties and with the material relations arising therefrom."[5] For workers, commodities appear "as what they really are, material relations between persons and social relations between things."[6] Commodity fetishism isn't a misunderstanding but "a consti-

3   Karl Marx, *Capital: A Critique of Political Economy (Vol. 1): The Process of Capitalist Production*, trans. S. Moore and E. Aveling (New York: International Publishers, 1867/1967), 77.

4   Don Mitchell, "A Complicated Fetish," *Social & Cultural Geography* 15, no. 2 (2014): 125.

5   Marx, *Capital (Vol. 1)*, 77.

6   Ibid., 78.

tutive aspect of the collective sensorium that has been socially constructed under capitalism" and "is value-laden and often unconscious."[7] Ideology is neither false consciousness nor is it, as Allman argues, "a defective way of thinking."[8] Commodity fetishism isn't about truthhood or falsehood; it is objectively *real*: commodities seem like "what they really are."

Even before the section on commodity fetishism, Marx establishes that "the value of commodities is the very opposite of the coarse materiality of their substance, not an atom of matter enters into its composition."[9] Value is not only defined as the socially-necessary labor time required to produce a given commodity, but as a sensual relationship Marx hears only by listening to the language commodities, for "the value of commodities [...] is told us by the linen itself, so soon as it comes into communication with another commodity, the coat."[10] Value—the lifeblood of capital—isn't immediately perceptible, as it "does not stalk about with a label describing what it is" but is an invisible presence "that converts every product into a social hieroglyphic."[11] Value is "purely social," although this objective sociality is incorporeal and can only be represented "by the totality of their social relations alone."[12] In another perceptual metaphor, Marx says value is only *represented* when commodities stand in relationship to each other, for it is only then that they take on the

---

7   Ponce de León and Rockhill, "Towards a Compositional Model of Ideology," 102.

8   Allman, *Critical Education Against Global Capitalism*, 42.

9   Marx, *Capital (Vol. 1)*, 54.

10   Ibid., 58.

11   Ibid., 79.

12   Ibid., 71.

form of "a mirror of value."[13] Commodity fetishism is a sensual process that results in a world where capital makes sense.

Capitalist ideology isn't imposed on us by the ruling class; on the contrary, it produces the forms through which capitalists themselves sense and understand the world. Take the general rate of profit from the third volume of *Capital*. Profit is different from surplus-value in that the former is the ratio of surplus over constant and variable capital while the latter is the ratio of surplus over variable capital. The capitalist doesn't distinguish between constant and variable capital and, "since in the rate of profit the surplus-value is calculated in relation to the total capital and the latter is taken as its standard of measurement, the surplus-value itself appears to originate from the total capital [...] Disguised as profit, surplus-value actually denies its origin, loses its character, and becomes unrecognisable."[14] Capitalist economists remain "at home in the estranged outward appearances of economic relations in which these *prima facie* absurd and perfect contradictions appear and that these relationships seem the more self-evident the more their internal relationships are concealed from it, although they are understandable to the popular mind."[15] As such, they can't identify either the differences between land, labor, or the social relation of value.

In the second volume of *Capital*, we see how bourgeois political economists and other capitalist apologists fall over themselves trying to understand the origins of profit. When Marx

---

13   Ibid., 64.

14   Karl Marx, *Capital: A Critique of Political Economy (Vol. 3): The Process of Capitalist Production as a Whole* (New York: International Publishers, 1894/1977), 167.

15   Ibid., 817.

breaks down the circulation of capital into three different phases in part one, he details the peculiarity of the circuit of money-capital. In this circuit, the production process appears as an *interruption*, "as a necessary evil for the sake of money-making," which is why "all nations with a capitalist mode of production are therefore seized periodically by a feverish attempt to make money without the intervention of the process of production."[16] It's similar to the wage in volume one. As a form of value, we sense the wage as payment for the entirety of our working time. "The wage-form," Marx discloses, "extinguishes every trace of the division of the working-day into necessary labour and surplus-labour, into paid and unpaid labour. All labour appears as paid labour." Value, which is imperceptible under capitalism, produces "this phenomenal form, which makes the actual relation invisible."[17] Making the social relations that collectivize us visible isn't a matter of pulling back the curtain but of transforming our practices of sight.

Consider Marx's note toward the end of volume three, that "if we strip both wages and surplus-value, both necessary and surplus labour, of their specifically capitalist character, then certainly there remain not these forms, but merely their rudiments, which are common to all social modes of production."[18] By eliminating the structure of capitalist accumulation, the phenomenal forms generated by capital can assume different roles in a new perceptual economy. Marx's proposal in volume two

---

16   Karl Marx, *Capital: A Critique of Political Economy (Vol. 2): The Process of Circulation of Capital* (New York: International Publishers, 1885/1967), 56.

17   Marx, *Capital (Vol. 1)*, 505.

18   Marx, *Capital (Vol. 3)*, 876.

is that "producers may, for all it matters, receive paper vouchers entitling them to withdraw from the social supplies of consumer goods a quantity corresponding to their labour-time."[19] These vouchers express a different social relation than money-capital and take on a different form insofar as they can't circulate, be bequeathed, used to buy means of production, etc.

As Marx makes clear, value as a social relation is "a secret," but "its discovery, while removing all appearance of mere accidentality from the determination of the magnitude of the values of products, yet in no way alters the mode in which that determination takes place."[20] Explanation and critique are imperative for revitalizing a collective revolutionary imaginary but are on their own insufficient if they aren't understood both as part of and relative to capital's overall perceptual ecology as it is reproduced through the totality of our everyday encounters and experiences. I see this most clearly expressed in the *Grundrisse*, where Marx registers that our labor is social in that it produces use-values for others, but "the social character of production is *posited* only *post festum* with the elevation of products to exchange values and the exchange of these exchange values."[21] Not only "the social character of activity" (labor), but also "the social form of the product" (or the commodity) take on an external form *and* content because "personal independence [is] founded on *objective* [...] dependence."[22] Our relations with each other *are* mediated through the exchange of commodities; hence, they *appear* as such! The problem with succumbing to the fetishistic

19   Marx, *Capital (Vol. 2)*, 358.

20   Marx, *Capital (Vol. 1)*, 80.

21   Marx, *Grundrisse*, 172.

22   Ibid., 157, 158.

appearances of capital is not so much that they hide the reality of exploitation but that they posit it as ahistorical and natural.

THE STRUGGLE FOR OTHER WORLDS

Teaching the actuality of revolution as an aesthetic, pedagogical, and political practice is important as our fight is, in part, a battle over "the socially forged sensory composition of a world," a fight for what Ponce de León refers to as an "other aesthetics," which names the production of a different social sensorium and a liberatory social order.[23] Capital and the struggle against it are aesthetic because they involve our senses of what makes or could make sense, because aesthetics pertains to "the production of experienced lifeworlds via material practices" taking place "within a complex social totality that is overdetermined by the social relations of production." The aesthetic element of the class struggle is, crucially, not limited to "art." Equating aesthetics with art obscures "the social force aesthetics exercises through other social practices."[24] In turn, it ignores other aesthetic manifestations and elevates the production of artworks as uniquely aesthetic.

Althusser gets at this in an interview on literary history where he pointedly asks art theorists: "How does it happen that such-and-such a work is considered to be, exists as, an aesthetic object?"[25] In the final instance, the operation works like this: workers in an advanced division of labor that includes literary specialists develop aesthetic categories that they then impose on the entire history of literature, a process through which they

23   Ponce de León, *Another Aesthetics is Possible*, 4.

24   Ibid., 5.

25   Louis Althusser, *History and Imperialism: Writings, 1963-1986*, trans. G.M. Goshgarian (Cambridge: Polity Press, 2018/2020), 7.

define what literature and the aesthetic are. Two decades on, he stresses again that aesthetic norms are "ideological relations of class struggle."[26] As a concept, the aesthetic is produced at determinate conjunctures for certain—and varying—purposes. The purpose of isolating "the aesthetic" and its norms of beauty, and so on, is to reinforce the idealist illusion that through the aesthetic we can reconcile class and other antagonisms.

Althusser intervenes in the battle over art by historicizing it and expressing that the artificial fragmentation of the totality into discrete domains was (and is) a historical production. Rockhill does the same through his methodology of radical history, which establishes that dominant studies on art and politics assume that both are clearly distinct, universal, and permanent entities that relate to each other when they meet at a specific and timeless intersection. Instead, what counts as art and politics—and the politics of art—are historically produced and determined through various struggles across space and time and by attending to processes of social production, distribution, and consumption. The "autonomy of art" thesis is the most striking proof offered. According to this thesis, "real," "true," or "authentic" art exists independently from political economy, as a sovereign thing that doesn't depend on any external justification or referent. Rockhill points out, however, that "the very idea that art could be autonomous from society is an oxymoron: it is itself a social category."[27] During the Cold War, for example, the CIA used the autonomy of art thesis in their struggle against communism. Because communist societies understood everything as

---

26   Louis Althusser, *Philosophy for Non-Philosophers*, trans. G.M. Goshgarian (London: Bloomsbury, 2014/2017), 154.

27   Rockhill, *Radical History and the Politics of Art*, 47.

political, the argument was that the detachment of art from political agendas proves the "freedom" of capitalist societies. The ultimate irony, then, is that "an art movement that was largely perceived to be apolitical became 'a prime political weapon.'"[28]

Rockhill's intervention is political as it participates in the struggle over defining art and politics, for *describing* intrudes into the struggle over both. Here, education assumes a central but unacknowledged role. Rockhill's project is pedagogical insofar as it involves "mapping out—and participating in—the dynamic interaction between multidimensional social practices."[29] The politics of art are not about the art object but the conditions of its production, distribution, and consumption, so we need to map these elements as they take place. This educational process has a different emphasis than what Ponce de León and Rockhill conceptualize at the end of their essay on ideology, where collective education proceeds by *demonstrating* alternative aesthetic worlds. Demonstration is a different educational endeavor than critique or explanation because "it is one thing to tell people that another world is possible; it is quite another to show them that another possible world is actual."[30] Education's political capacity emanates from producing encounters of sensual experiences beyond those of capital.

In Rockhill's earlier book, mapping is a process of investigating and discovering the myriad social forces at work in the production, distribution, and reception of what's designated as "art" and "politics," whereas in his later work with Ponce de

---

28   Ibid., 216.

29   Ibid., 50.

30   Ponce de León and Rockhill, "Towards a Compositional Model of Ideology," 110.

León, collective education is aesthetic insofar as it *shows* a different aesthetic and political world is possible through *experiencing* the force of alternative modes of representation, ways of sensing, and so on. This book primarily takes up this latter call by analyzing the educational dynamics and pedagogical logics that reproduce capital's perceptual ecology and by proposing others that can intervene in the production of an alternative sensorium or another aesthetics. It's not that description is unimportant or categorically distinct from demonstration, but that it's overemphasized in marxist educational theory at the expense of demonstration.

Like politics and art, the concepts and practices of pedagogy and politics are contingent on place, time, and the balance of forces. Before articulating educational dynamics that reproduce, and challenge, the perceptual ecology of capital in our contemporary conjuncture, I want to weave together the elements proposed so far by outlining the *pedagogy* of Marx's method of presentation in *Capital* as a whole, reading Marx's first preface to *Capital*, his critique of *so-called* primitive accumulation, and returning to the fetishism of commodities to synthesize the argument. The aesthetic pedagogy at work in Marx is *political*, by which I mean the various tactics he deploys—from brief metaphors to extended quotations—are part of his overall political strategy of theoretical articulation and not due to literary preferences or flourishes.

Aesthetic Pedagogy: So-Called Primitive Accumulation

In the preface for the first edition of *Capital*, Marx states "it is the ultimate aim of this work, to lay bare the economic law of motion of modern society," a social formation in which the capitalist mode of production is dominant.[31] All social formations are combinations of different modes of production and in any given social formation, time, space, and labor are uneven. "In all forms of society," as he puts it in the *Grundrisse*, "there is one specific kind of production which predominates over the rest, whose relations thus assign rank and influence to the others [...] Capital is the all-dominating economic power of bourgeois society."[32] Delineating between social formations and modes of production clarifies that various modes of production, temporalities, and spatial relations coexist in any given society (although one will always be dominant or striving for dominance) and produce different social relations and antagonisms, landscapes, and possibilities.

England serves "as the *chief* illustration" in *Capital* because it was where "the natural laws of capitalist production" were most dominant over other modes of production and were more observable.[33] At the same time, England still suffered from "a whole series of inherited evils [...] arising from the passive survival of antiquated modes of production" together with "modern evils."[34] He prefaces the first volume by clearly stating both the objective of the work and the ultimate impossibility of that objective in that he can only discern the "natural laws" of capital by examining a concrete social formation. Even these "natural

31   Marx, *Capital (Vol. 1)*, 20.

32   Marx, *Grundrisse*, 106-107.

33   Marx, *Capital (Vol. 1)*, 19, emphasis added. Marx also turns to England because "the social statistics of Germany and the rest of Continental Western Europe are, in comparison [...] wretchedly compiled." Ibid., 20.

34   Ibid., 20.

laws" are, as he repeatedly reminds the reader, adjusted in their actual operation.[35]

In the concluding part of the first volume, Marx explains that capital's development in England resulted from its location within the global balance of forces—as a *colonial state* power. Marx attributes the status of English capital to, among other things, "conquest, enslavement, robbery, murder," national and international debts, the enclosure of the commons and the violent disciplining of peasants into wage laborers, "the discovery of gold and silver," "the extirpation, enslavement and entombment in mines of the aboriginal population," "the conquest and looting of the East Indies, the turning of Africa into a warren for the commercial hunting of black skins," and "slavery pure and simple" in the United States.[36]

The most general reading of this section, referred to as Marx's account of "primitive accumulation," presents it as a universal and finalized origin story of capitalism.[37] This not only discloses a lack of attention to this section and the text overall that maintains the break in ideological continuity of the people's movements, but it also distorts his overall conception of capital insofar as Marx's explanation of capitalist development in England is part of his account of how capital produces (and

35   This is most evident when, just after he spells out "the absolute general law of capitalist accumulation," he clarifies that "like all other laws it is modified in its working by many circumstances." Ibid., 603.

36   Ibid., 668, 703, 711.

37   For the most widely cited examples of this misreading, see Cedric Robinson, *Black Marxism: The Making of the Black Radical Tradition* (Chapel Hill: The University of North Carolina Press, 1983/2000); and David Harvey, "The 'New' Imperialism: Accumulation by Dispossession," *Socialist Register* 40 (2004): 63-87.

reproduces) its own natural laws. I address these related errors, in turn, not only to correct them but, by doing so, to demonstrate how *Capital*'s aesthetic pedagogy teaches the actuality of revolution.

Marx's conception of capital doesn't entail primitive accumulation but rather, as part 8 is titled, "The So-Called Primitive Accumulation." He introduces it with these words:

> We have seen how money is changed into capital; how through capital surplus-value is made, and from surplus-value more capital. But the accumulation of capital pre-supposes surplus-value; surplus-value pre-supposes capitalist production; capitalistic production pre-supposes the pre-existence of considerable masses of capital and of labour-power in the hands of producers of commodities. The whole movement, therefore, seems to turn in a vicious circle, out of which we can only get by *supposing* a primitive accumulation.[38]

He likens it to "original sin" because the entire process through which capital produces and reproduces itself (and hence its laws) can only be theorized by repeatedly supposing an origin outside of capital. "The so-called primitive accumulation," he writes, "is nothing else than the historical process of divorcing the producer from the means of production. It *appears* as primitive because it forms the pre-historic stage of capital."[39] Because capital's reproduction is a "vicious circle," however, this pre-history must necessarily repeat itself and, to do so, must continue to function like the myth of original sin.

The reproduction of capital's perceptual ecology revolves around a pre-history that is continually present. Capital must

---

38   Marx, *Capital (Vol. 1)*, 667, emphasis added.

39   Ibid., 668, emphasis added.

perpetually cover over its "untraceable and repeating origin," as Gavin Walker spells out, "by 'presupposing' its own 'suppositions,' capital acts in such a way as to ensure that its limits are sealed off" as capital produces a conception of time where it is natural and permanent, recurrently producing "itself up from a history that it inscribes back onto the historical process."[40] The misreading of primitive accumulation as a finished origin story of capital thus *reinforces* capital's erasure of its ongoing dispossession and works to create the anti-communist "Left" that's acceptable to capital. More to my point, it distorts Marx's different research techniques and presentational styles by erecting, as David Harvey does, an "unbridgeable divide" in marxism between theory and history, where "Marx views 'history' on the one hand and economics and the critique of political economy on the other as two distinguishable, if not separate, fields of enquiry."[41] This distortion, in turn, prevents the aesthetic pedagogy of *Capital* from teaching the actuality of revolution as it weaves the ongoing gaps in the temporality and rationality of capital's perceptual ecology together.

The preface with which Marx begins the book ends by listing a series of ongoing struggles. These battles "are signs of the times" illustrating "that, within the ruling-classes themselves, a foreboding is dawning, that the present society is no solid crystal, but an organism capable of change, and is constantly

---

40   Gavin Walker, *The Sublime Perversion of Capital: Marxist Theory and the Politics of History in Modern Japan* (Durham: Duke University Press, 2016), 12, 22.

41   David Harvey, "History Versus Theory: A Commentary on Marx's Method in *Capital*," *Historical Materialism* 20, no. 2 (2012): 4.

changing."[42] Ending the book by showing how capital's ongoing—brutal and state-imposed—origins are repeatedly created
and erased demonstrates that capital's narrative of itself is constantly interrupted by alternatives, opening up a space in which
oppositional forces can intervene.

AESTHETIC PEDAGOGY: COMMODITY FETISHISM

Articulating the logic of capital and arming our class requires transforming our cognition and sensation, which I think
explains Marx's hesitation over publishing the French translation
as a series of separate articles in progressive newspapers between
1872-75. His 1872 letter to the publisher, Maurice Lachâtre,
expresses both approval and worry. "I applaud your idea of publishing the translation of *Capital* as a serial," he says, as this will
make it "more accessible to the working class, a consideration
which to me outweighs everything else." At the same time, because it would appear piecemeal over time, he "feared" readers
"may be disheartened" by the incapacity to link "the immediate
questions that have *aroused* their passions" with their "general
principles"—as a result of the specific form of the book's publication and, hence, distribution, exchange, and consumption.[43]

The first volume of *Capital* is the only one Marx published
(and republished) in his lifetime, and throughout the different
publications and translations, he (and Engels) constantly wres-
tle with how the book's presentation could most effectively explain and inspire the class struggle. One of the significant changes Marx chose to make was the addition of the section on the
fetishism of commodities, which didn't appear until the early

42   Marx, *Capital (Vol. 1)*, 21.

43   Ibid., 30.

1870s with the second German and first French editions.[44] In the German edition's afterword, Marx comments on the book's educational logics, clarifying that "the method of presentation must differ in form from that of inquiry," as the method of inquiry examines the educational content "in detail, to analyse its different forms of development, to trace out their inner connexion" while the method of presentation must, after inquiry is over, appropriately portray the object of study.[45] Marx was indisputably thinking about how the *pedagogy* of *Capital* can render its content *sensible*, can advance the struggles of working and oppressed peoples, so it's noteworthy that, in the end, he decided to conclude the first chapter with this section that interrupts the flow of his elaboration of value (which could have simply moved from the general or money-form of value to exchange).

Intriguingly, this section contains the first mention of communism in *Capital* (and the only one in the first several chapters), and Marx's form of presentation moves from analytical argumentation to literary analysis and allusion. This shift makes it possible for us to sense the social reality of value, the perceptual ecology of capital, and the actuality of revolution. As we reflect on reality, the substance of capitalist commodity production has "already acquired the stability of natural, self-understood forms of social life."[46] We can only get value as a social relation

---

44   Between sending the manuscript off and its actual publication, Marx briefly wrote an appendix that referenced commodity fetishism. The concept also crops up in earlier notebooks, like the section of the *Grundrisse* cited above.

45   Ibid., 28. For more on these logics, see Derek R. Ford, *Encountering Education: Elements for a Marxist Pedagogy* (Madison: Iskra Books, 2022).

46   Marx, *Capital (Vol. 1)*, 80.

corresponding to capital by historicizing it, so Marx visits other modes of production. Beginning with Daniel Defoe's *Robinson Crusoe*, a favorite of the political economists, we "transport ourselves from Robinson's island bathed in light to the European middle ages shrouded in darkness" *en route* to patriarchal and communal labor and, finally, the communist mode of production.[47] "Let us now picture to ourselves," he implores, "a community of free individuals, carrying on their work with the means of production in common, in which the labor-power of all the different individuals is consciously applied as the combined labor-power of the community" results in a "social product" collectively owned and distributed.[48] We can only *imagine* such a mode of production. It is not as if under communism I'll walk into the grocery store and the complex processes that brought the items there will be rendered visible and accessible, or as if the communist struggle is a process of articulating and critiquing such processes. We can't even know what subjectivity will look like once social production organizes society as a presupposition rather than as mediated through commodity exchange.

The argument's aesthetic mode coincides with its content because the commodity (under capitalism) is a "common, every-day thing" and "something transcendent," something standing "with its feet on the ground" as well as "on its head."[49] His presentation establishes a theory of immaterial value and an impression of the communist future that develops—and breaks down—throughout the argument, especially once we get to the class struggle. The method is neither closed nor self-referential;

47   Ibid., 81.
48   Ibid., 82-83.
49   Ibid., 76.

it is contingent, open, and subject to the class struggle as Marx "takes his own theory into account by politically *posing* and *exposing his own ideas*."[50] The section on the fetishism of commodities, which glosses over the history of different modes of production, is one place Marx transitions from the certainty of calculation and arithmetic for the uncertainty of historical practice and anticipatory imagination and, by doing so, represents the historical production of arithmetic certainty itself. The section on *so-called* primitive accumulation, for its part, represents the particular situations in which we can struggle to alter and overthrow capital's general operations by highlighting their contingent and historical nature.

Capital is, as a result, not an exclusively "theoretical" text that's interrupted or juxtaposed with history or politics, nor does it pursue, as Gayatri Spivak thinks, the "positive task of acquiring the rational x-ray vision that would cut through the fetish-character of the commodity."[51] By exposing his investigation to an encounter with the outside instead of articulating a neat and logical conclusion, Marx's pedagogy *enacts* the contingencies of class struggle. The communist project conditions its pedagogy as Marx helps us understand capital's contradictions and weak points, know the collectivity that capital abstracts us from repeatedly, and *sense* the coexistence of future possibilities within the present.

---

50   Louis Althusser, *Philosophy of the Encounter: Later Writings, 1978-1987*, trans. G.M. Goshgarian (New York: Verso, 1993/2006), 47.

51   Gayatri Chakravorty Spivak, *A Critique of Postcolonial Reason: Toward a History of the Vanishing Present* (Cambridge: Harvard University Press, 1999), 75, note 97.

CHAPTER 2

TEACHING AS UNLEARNING ANOTHER AESTHETIC

We're wedded to capital's perceptual ecology educationally. If we can experiment with alternative pedagogies for the revolutionary struggle, then it makes sense to turn to Freire, who expressly builds the pedagogical dynamics and even practices for revolutionary education. For Freire, "revolution undeniably has an educational nature" and "the taking of power is only one moment—no matter how decisive—in the revolutionary process."[1] His pedagogical theories are weapons for revolutionary organizations. Because "the revolution is made neither by the leaders for the people, nor by the people for the leaders, but by both acting together in unshakable solidarity," Freire's pedagogy is the hinge between the party and the masses.[2] Structured by the party, the cultural and political revolution advances through

---

1 Paulo Freire, *Pedagogy of the Oppressed*, trans. M.B. Ramos (New York: Continuum, 1970/2011), 136.

2 Ibid., 129.

dialogic pedagogical processes before, during, and after taking power.

Dialogical pedagogy is organized around generative themes or limit-situations, settings in which people are "directed at negating and overcoming, rather than passively accepting, the 'given.'"[3] As we saw in the last chapter, under capitalism the given world takes the form of *objects* separated from social processes of production. Dialogical pedagogy confronts the given by critically analyzing (decoding) objects or events as part of larger and shifting totalities. In *Pedagogy of the Oppressed*, Freire gives the sketch or photograph as an example of "a coded existential situation" reproducing our perception of the world as a combination of distinct and autonomous lifeless objects by appearing as an autonomous entity.[4] Through dialogue, we decode the codified object and experience and understand ourselves and each other as active agents in the construction of our world. Freire's *Education for Critical Consciousness* extends the decoding process through the "culture circle," a space where participants discuss, analyze, and clarify cultural objects as parts of a larger totality and then create plans to act on their findings. The cultural circle is "a program which itself would be an act of creation, capable of releasing other creative acts."[5] The book provides 10 carefully curated images that move participants through the decoding process to advance critical consciousness. When we get to the last image, "the Culture Circle participants easily identify them-

---

3   Ibid., 99.

4   Ibid., 105.

5   Paulo Freire, *Education for Critical Consciousness* (London: Continuum, 1974/2015), 41.

selves."[6]

Here we run up against a contradiction in Freire's pedagogy. Freire positions the images as visually coded messages whose intended meanings we can know through a progressive decoding. As such, "there is a clear correlation between the intention of the artist/author, the visual representation (the code), and the interpretation of the students (de-coding)."[7] This is incompatible with Freire's desire for students to become active participants in constructing the world for "creation in this mode is never the creation of the new, nor is agency the agency of invention, and the word appears as the result of an ideal causality that translates intentions to images and signs."[8] Freire's pedagogy remains trapped within the *intended message* of the object or artwork through a dialogue depleted only by "reaching a predetermined, final destination determined by a pre-existing intention."[9] Because the reception of the artwork or cultural object is predetermined, this pedagogy lacks the possibility of experiencing other potential modalities of perception and forecloses the pedagogical opening to unlearning another aesthetics.

LEARNING: THE MOTOR OF CAPITAL'S PERCEPTUAL ECOLOGY

In the ongoing privatization of education in the U.S., the arts are often first on the chopping block. Their supporters primarily occupy a defensive position, justifying art on its *utility* to

---

6   Ibid., 77.

7   Tyson E. Lewis, *The Aesthetics of Education: Theatre, Curiosity, and Politics in the Work of Jacques Rancière and Paulo Freire* (London: Bloomsbury, 2012), 140.

8   Ibid.

9   Ibid., 144.

the economy, the nation, and education, positioning the arts as *tools* to improve other educational outcomes. Others fight for funding art education on the basis that aesthetic appreciation produces the intellectual, social, emotional, entrepreneurial, collaborative, and other skills necessary for learning, education, employment, and life in general. In each case, art education is defended *within* the capitalist regime of value and becomes a chief *means* to achieve external ends, reinforcing the logic of capital and subjecting the arts to other disciplines ("learn music because it'll make you better at math"). They double down and reinforce the same processes that defund art in the first place, as each places art at the service of something else. Opposed to the instrumentalization of the arts in education, some defend the value of art for art's sake. Appealing to the autonomy of art thesis, they prioritize the subjective pleasure that comes from engaging with beautiful artworks, the enculturation of young people and other students, etc. The aesthetic is set aside as a distinct area or domain that supplements education.

Missed in each approach is the question of how education is, *by definition*, aesthetic in that it always rests upon, reinforces, or challenges dominant regimes of perception, or hegemonic ways of seeing, feeling, smelling, hearing, and tasting. The aesthetic isn't an *addition* to education; it is "an aesthetic experience that teaches us to redistribute the relationship between what can and cannot be seen as well as what can and cannot be heard."[10] If (aesthetic) education necessarily integrates us into certain perceptual organizations of society, and if modes of production and social formations—and the struggles for and against different ones—are always partly about the organization of what and how

---

10   Ibid., 9.

we sense and make sense of the world, how should we understand the relationships between education, political struggles, and aesthetics?

The question for me as an educational theorist, teacher, and organizer is: what is the educational project of the class struggle? How does—or how *might*—education strengthen our political movements by attending to the aesthetics of pedagogy? Is it a matter of teaching the right political orientations and aesthetic theories? Is it a matter of inquiring into how, why, and by what forces something becomes assigned to the realm or level of political "culture" or "art" by describing the composition of the social forces behind this assignment, a description which would then change the contours of that struggle? To answer the question, we first need to think education in terms of *pedagogy* instead of content. This is not to undervalue the content taught, which is critical in education and can take political priority over pedagogy, but to call our attention to the often neglected question of form in the marxist tradition. The pedagogical forms through which we engage others in revolutionary content are absolutely central because "even the most revolutionary, relevant and accessible content can be engaged in a way that turns people off, shuts them down or otherwise disengages them."[11] This doesn't mean that we can designate certain pedagogical forms as inherently and universally revolutionary or even marxist. Who among us, to take the classic example of the "monological" lecture, hasn't been thoroughly aroused, inspired, and *educated* by a speech giv-

---

11   Liberation School Editorial Collective, "Introduction: Revolutionary Education and the Promotion of Socialist Consciousness," in N. Brown (ed.), *Revolutionary Education: Theory and Practice for Socialist Organizers*, 2nd ed. (San Francisco: Liberation Media, 2022), ix.

en at a forum or protest, conference or picket line?

What are the educational elements of our current conjuncture? One place to start is noting how teaching has been redefined as—and reduced to—the facilitation of learning. The language of education, teaching, students, schools, and universities is almost totally supplanted by "the language and discourse of learning."[12] This is a real material, political, and aesthetic shift intimately tied up with—and determined by—the mode of production. Because learning is "the actualization of an intention that can be quantified in relation to a goal" it "is an economy, a management of potentiality in the name of future measure and the promise of improvement."[13] The economy of learning resounds with—or is the educational pivot of—the contemporary dominance of finance capital, as it is governed according to the effective "administration of resources and funds, the minimization of risk through calculation, and an investment into human capital development, all with the goal of future productivity in mind."[14] In the learning economy, we are individuals compelled to endlessly identify, improve, accumulate, and perform our competencies as we engage in the life-and-death struggle to sell our labor-power in the flexible global marketplace of capital.

Through this aesthetic induction into capitalism, we learn to sacrifice again and again so we can learn and relearn skills, knowledges, habits, worldviews, ways of thinking, orientations, dispositions, and even bodily comportments to remain competitive in the struggle for survival. We learn as fast as possible,

12   Biesta, *The Beautiful Risk of Education*, 59.

13   Tyson E. Lewis, *Inoperative Learning: A Radical Rewriting of Educational Potentialities* (New York: Routledge, 2018), 2.

14   Ibid., 3-4.

racing through coursework structured by learning "goals" and "outcomes." We learn about what exists to generate new insights about it and birth something *new* into existence, to *master* and *discover* something novel. Again, this isn't by choice: we keep learning because we're never sure if we'll have a job tomorrow or not.

We learn to sense knowledge as a commodity—as an external and distinct object with a use-value and exchange-value we can acquire or transmit—instead of as a social relation between diverse segments of subjects in the global working class distributed across time and space unevenly. We learn what to see as we learn what's invisible, what to listen for as we learn what's inaudible, what can touch us as we learn what can't. We learn *common sense*, acquiring the wisdom to judge not only what and how to see, but what is and isn't worthy of vision, how to prioritize good sights and bad sights—what *should* and *shouldn't* enter the sensuous field according to the general law of capitalist accumulation. We not only learn what we *shouldn't* hear but *how* to not hear certain sounds.

As a capitalist pedagogy, learning produces subjects who—to varying degrees—fit with the capitalist "modeling of perceptions, feelings, habits, actions, memories, and desire."[15] We perceive education itself as the endless production of ever-differentiated forms of labor-power and attune our habits and actions to the latest needs of capital. These ends determine what classes we take, what majors we pursue, where and if we go to school, what and how we teach, etc. The degree to which we actualize certain potentials determines our location in capital's totality. For example, literacy hasn't always determined the worthiness

---

15   Ponce de León, *Another Aesthetics is Possible*, 5.

or employability of people. Literacy (and illiteracy) only began determining who can and can't work, vote, reproduce, and so on, with the spread of industrial capitalism (and the printing press).[16]

Guided solely by the need to actualize and accumulate as quickly and efficiently as possible, the pedagogy of learning explains the recent uptick in concerns about "learning disabilities," including the market race to identify, treat, and correct or eliminate disabilities, at least in those who have demonstrated their *potential* to overcome them.[17] Those disabled by capitalism "must be made productive or expendable."[18] Some students make "good investments" and others are clearly "bad risks," and resources should be redistributed from the latter to the former to improve educational outcomes and returns. In turn, students perceive and relate to teachers as customer service representatives that are tasked with meeting their demands and living up to the learner's expectations. The spreading and increasing importance of student opinion surveys in higher education evidence that even teaching is framed through the capitalist logic of learning.

Our mental and physical relations to the world are structured through capitalist ideology via the economy of learning. We discern what is possible and impossible along the lines of

16   Jay Timothy Dolmage, *Academic Ableism: Disability and Higher Education* (Ann Arbor: University of Michigan Press, 2017).

17   Megha Summer Pappachen and Derek R. Ford, "Spreading Stupidity: Disability and Anti-Imperialist Resistance to Bio-Informational Capitalism," in M.A. Peters, P. Jandrić, and S. Hayes (eds.), *Bioinformational Philosophy and Postdigital Knowledge Ecologies* (New York: Springer, 2022).

18   Dolmage, *Academic Ableism*, 108.

this world based on commodified theories available through academic and other knowledge institutions. It makes sense, then, to channel desires for a more equitable and just world into the circuits of capitalist production and exchange, to produce new and better knowledge commodities. We learn to feel the world as a composition of already actualized practices. To intensify and increase accumulation, learning reinforces what Ariella Aïsha Azoulay terms the "right to discover, uncover, penetrate, scrutinize, copy, and appropriate."[19] The goal of learning is to bring—or take—something from the outside into *our* understanding, accumulating more and more of the world by integrating it into the capitalist regime of sense-making. The successful learner is one who "mastered" some worldly phenomenon according to the global imperative of capitalist competition, an educational manifestation of *so-called* primitive accumulation.

The way to pursue our desires is based on the ideology of the individual; these aren't *our* desires but *my* ambitions. The capitalist aesthetic regime produces the individual form of the subject. Although capitalist production is globally socialized, we receive *individual* wages, not collective ones. Through the wage—which we receive in exchange for our labor-power—we're abstracted as individuals. Only with capitalism do "individuals come into connection with one another only in determined ways," such that "individuals are now ruled by *abstractions*, whereas earlier they depended on one another."[20] As learning drives contemporary capital, learning is individualized, so it just makes sense that *my* labor-power has to be different

19   Ariella Aïsha Azoulay, *Potential History: Unlearning Imperialism* (New York: Verso. 2019), 53.

20   Marx, *Grundrisse*, 164.

from yours, that *my* theory has to be different from (and better than) *yours.*

The above definition of the individual appears early in the chapter on money in Marx's *Grundrisse* because value is a real abstraction that governs subjectivity and social relations. Money is the tangible abstract representation of an intangible abstraction, value. Money dissolves or disrupts the relations in which it intervenes because "it is indifferent to its particularity and takes on every form which serves the purpose" so that "where money is not itself the community [...] it must dissolve the community."[21] The capitalist mode of production produces us as subjects who sense ourselves and each other as fragmented individuals pursuing autonomous interests, rather than as collectives or classes each participating in—and determined by—a larger totality. Capital produces the fragmented individual *because* there is such a high degree of social connectivity.

Our social bond is produced by a world organized around the production of value. It is only "in the developed system of exchange" that "the ties of personal dependence [...] are in fact exploded, ripped up [...] and individuals *seem* independent [...] but they appear thus only for someone who abstracts from the *conditions*, the *conditions of existence* within which these individuals enter into contact."[22] The reproduction of capital's perceptual regime isn't a matter of a bad curriculum, inadequate or outdated texts, faulty reasoning, a lack of critical thinking skills, or, as the global industry bemoans, a closing of the public sphere; it's a matter of the *pedagogy of learning.* It's not something we can *improve* because such an improvement would reinforce cap-

---

21   Ibid., 224.

22   Ibid., 163-164.

ital's logic. Learning and the learner are produced by the structural conditions of capital, a system that increasingly fragments our world, placing each of us into an overarching scheme of production whose totality exceeds our imaginative, cognitive, and sensory possibilities. Capital's perceptual ecology functions through an aesthetic education resting upon and reinforcing our senses of subjectivity in the form of individuality, education in the form of a colonial expedition of discovery, and the possible and impossible in the form of commodities. By channeling our indignation and responses into capital's logic, learning limits the possibility of *imagining* and *creating* a radically different world through collective revolutionary struggle.

UNLEARNING: AESTHETIC PEDAGOGY FOR CLASS STRUGGLE

To foster a collective imaginary beyond capital we need to engage in epistemological critique, developing thorough and intricate analyses and providing clear explanations to others. We also need to experience aesthetic encounters beyond the contemporary order. Critique, description, and aesthetic encounters are educational, and my goal is to further enunciate some pedagogical possibilities we can experiment with as we cultivate this imaginary. If the contemporary learning apparatus inaugurates us into the perceptual ecology of capital, it follows that we should develop alternative pedagogical forms and practices that sensually and cognitively expose the limits of our present imaginary and induce sensations of an alternative world in the present. I begin by characterizing teaching not as an act that facilitates learning but as one that promotes *unlearning*. Teaching is a practice that, by *pointing*, provokes, opens, and maintains the spaces and times required for *unlearning* capital's world-form to experience the possibility of a different perceptual ecology.

To reclaim it from the domination of learning, Biesta holds that education is *defined* by teaching and that teaching is fundamentally constituted by *pointing*. He maintains that "the basic gesture of teaching as that of *redirecting someone else's* gaze."[23] The teacher points in two ways simultaneously: they point *at* a student by pointing the student *to* some *thing*. What is the syllabus but an example of such pointing, insofar as the syllabus points the students' gaze to purposive content? Teaching calls students to attend to the intended content in precise moments for a definite reason. Because teaching is distinct from learning, there are no predetermined ends the student has to reach nor, as a result, is there any "progress" the teacher can measure.

As any teacher knows, this gesture only allows for the *possibility* that students will take up that which is pointed to. Regardless of any "teacher-proof" curriculum they develop, teaching is never anything more than a possibility without guarantees. Nothing can secure an outcome or ensure the student responds to the pointing and redirects their gaze (or even recognizes the teacher's call). Even with the power of grading, I can only ever *try* to have students encounter me, each other, the syllabus, and the world. Even with other, less capitalist means, like building trust and collectively producing the classroom atmosphere, there's no getting around the fact that we can (and do) refuse to engage for a multitude of reasons.

Teaching derives its educational force from the teacher's intention to engage singular and collective students in certain content and derives its political force from the teacher's aim to

---

23   Gert J.J. Biesta, *World-Centered Education: A View for the Present* (New York: Routledge, 2022), 77.

point *specific* student(s) to *politically* curated content at *distinctive* moments in the educational process as determined by the conjuncture. Teaching as the facilitation of *unlearning* is aesthetic as it opens fissures within the world as it is, inaugurating a break in learning and interrupting the dominant sensorium. The "moments of breakdown" the teacher arranges disclose "a perceptual space wherein things can shine forth."[24] Unlearning "enables a gap to emerge through which things can appear (no matter how briefly or indirectly)" and that, accordingly, "dis-orients us, and thus opens up a new access point."[25] By producing the conditions for an unforeseen encounter, unlearning can break open an experience of being "in-between" the world as it is and as it could be. Unlearning puts us off our course, setting us adrift, suspending the perceptual ecology of capital, and making room for the development of an alternative sensorium. Teaching the actuality of revolution demands unlearning insofar as it's a pedagogy predicated upon obeying the cracks between the present conjuncture and the revolution; not one that tries to *close* or *answer* the void between the two, but one that helps us experience the possibility that defines any revolutionary transformation.

If learning is about discovering something new, then unlearning is about another aesthetic relationship, one in which we're subjected to the gaps in the present to unlearn our relationship with the world organized by capital's perceptual ecology. We notice we're unlearning when that which seemed so familiar suddenly seems uncertain and strange, when an ideo-

---

24 Tyson E. Lewis, "The Pedagogical Power of Things: Toward a Post-Intentional Phenomenology of Unlearning," *Cultural Critique* 98, Winter: 130.

25 Ibid., 132.

logical framework or worldview that seemed so total, natural, and timeless suddenly appears as the result and condition of historical processes. To that end, unlearning is "*undiscovering*," unlearning "the quest for the new that drives academic disciplines."[26] Marxist pedagogy teaches us to unlearn by interrupting learning's drive to effortlessly and without delay make sense of something. Because internalizing the world into our existing sense-making is the educational form of accumulation that reinforces students as colonial individuals collecting knowledge and experience from an external and completed history, it precludes our sensation of the constant eruption of the past in the present. In the *time* of unlearning, the past and future turn up as present.

Because teaching is independent of learning and not driven by the desires of learners, the gesture of teaching necessarily involves *force*. No longer guiding the learner in their efforts to acquire and master, students are forced to encounter the teacher's knowledge–which was previously external to the students–to let it disturb them and their sense of sense-making. When learning, we express *our* new understanding of an object; when unlearning, we experience an interruption in our sense-making and let the content disorient our understanding. The difference turns on the distinction between *understanding*—in which we accommodate a different experience into our cognition or, more broadly, feel it within the confines of our aesthetic legibility—and *encountering*—in which we experience the limits of our faculty to know and understand through our *inability* to make sense. Such moments of breakdown transform our perceptual regime and promote a radical collective imaginary. The educative gesture of pointing calls the student's attention to

26   Azoulay, *Potential History*, 16.

something outside of themselves, to an *opening* that can affect, disorder, and produce a misfit between the educational subjects and objects in a manner that's temporarily opaque, nonsensical. The opening interrupts the linearity of learning, preventing the accumulation of knowledge, the continuation of development, or the discovery of something new.

Ponce de León's analysis of "Mexican Laundry," a poem by Ricardo A. Bracho that intervenes in struggles over gentrification in Los Angeles, offers an example of the pedagogy of unlearning. The poem is inscribed on a plaque commemorating a downtown bar that fell victim to capital's cycles of investment and disinvestment. Gentrification is often framed as a visual transformation that takes place by destroying (killing) and rehabilitating (imprisoning) "unsightly" people and objects, constructing new buildings, parks, monuments, houses, and so on, to make them more "appealing." Surprisingly, the poem doesn't *articulate* the community, or parts and forms of the community, erased through gentrification. Because there are no written depictions of what existed before the influx of capital into the neighborhood, the poem "suggests a refusal to represent" what is displaced "in a way that would be easily assimilated to ideological uses of the visual." Instead of a textual representation of the visual, the poem uses "the phrase 'close eyes,'" which is "a refusal of the written text itself" that's "followed by an appeal to 'breath[e] beneath/[...] and smell." [27] The sense of sight through the eye moves to other perceptual capacities so we can *feel* the past in the present, the alternative that exists in the world as it is; the community that can never be eliminated.

The linearity of learning is interrupted as we unlearn our

---

27   Ponce de León, *Another Aesthetics is Possible*, 123.

dominant conception of temporality and encounter the variegated times that co-exist at any given moment. The poem's refusal to articulate determinate content for learning "treats the senses as a social phenomenon and decenters the individual subject in the act of constructing memory, so that the act of memory comes to appear as a latent potential embedded in places and their sensorial landscapes."[28] We anticipate the plaque to serve as a historical representation to discover and learn from, but we encounter an unexpected kink that detours the economy of learning. Preventing the accumulation of knowledge and the acquisition of a specific message, "Mexican Laundry" provokes unlearning through its refusal of decodability, its resistance to easy comprehension and internalization. Bracho's poem shouts, "*You*! Look *here*!" directing our attention to something we can't identify or incorporate into our self-development, prompting a challenge to our easy sense-making. When pointed to as political and educational matters, objects like Bracho's poem anticipate another perceptual ecology, making the current one strange and, in the same sweep, allowing us to unlearn capital's perceptual ecology.

REMEMBERING THE CONJUNCTURE

Aesthetics and what we struggle to constitute as political art are strategic points of intervention. Even the extent to which other acts of political contestation—like strikes and mass demonstrations—should focus on aesthetics is contingent upon various determinations we're intervening in and the agenda for which we're struggling.[29] Even as we can't move beyond the cap-

---

28   Ibid.

29   The idea of mass actions as perceptual educational experiences

italist aesthetic regime without abolishing the value form, the aesthetic educational process of unlearning proposed here could be a useful pedagogical weapon in the class struggle. Like any educational form, unlearning isn't revolutionary in an abstract sense that holds for all historical situations.

Unlearning shouldn't be valorized at the expense of learning *in general*, or without attending to the spaces, times, and political elements of the class struggle. The real issue at hand is *what* aesthetic economy we unlearn, for what reasons, and to what effect. I want to be clear that I'm not valorizing "interruption" uncritically or as politically productive in themselves, thanks to a lesson Sandy Grande's *Red Pedagogy* teaches. The lives of Indigenous nations and peoples in North America are already subjected to constant ruptures, as are the lives of oppressed and working people more generally. Grande's Red pedagogy consequently "embraces an educative process that works to reenchant the universe, to reconnect peoples to the land, and is as much about belief and acquiescence as it is about questioning and empowerment."[30] Instead of trying to break from traditions, Grande's pedagogy produces, delineates, and preserves a connection with them. Because the rupture of unlearning is a rupture within capitalism and colonialism, it can create a place and time in which tradition isn't relegated to a completed history but where it impresses its force on the present.

The pedagogical breakdowns of unlearning are encounters with another form of wealth. When we eradicate "the limited bourgeois form" of wealth, as Marx insists at one point, wealth

---

comes from Simon Boxley, "ESC in the Anthropocene: Education for Sustainability and Communism," *Critical Education* 13, no. 1 (2022): 51-69.

30   Grande, *Red Pedagogy*, 243.

will entail the absolute exploration of our "creative potentialities, with no presuppositions other than the previous historic development."[31] The wealth of unlearning isn't measured by value but spread by the experience of our potentiality divorced from the demand to actualize or perform within not only the current organization of perception but also, as we'll turn to in the next chapter, the capitalist framework of knowledge.

---

31   Marx, *Grundrisse*, 488.

CHAPTER 3

ENCOUNTERS WITH THE MATERIALITY OF THOUGHT

The collective experience of other potentials within the present and the cultivation of a radical imaginary challenge dominant theories of knowledge. Under capitalism, knowledge is fragmented and commodified, packaged and distributed for maximum efficiency, and the product of the singular human agent. Teaching the actuality of revolution today imposes a struggle over what's called "epistemology," which comes from two Greek words: "epistēmē" (or knowledge) and "logos" (or reason). The pedagogy and aesthetics of class struggle run up against the question of how and in whose interests we define knowledge and rationality. In this chapter, I contend that Emily Jean Hood and Tyson E. Lewis' concept of "thin(g)king" represents a form and practice of thought that challenges and might reorder capitalist modalities. Their research method aims at studying the relationships between humans and other matter, and they name it "thin(g)king" since it combines thinking and thing. Under "other matter," or what they call "more-than-human" materiality, they include "all material things, objects, and stuff, while also hinting at how such materiality is interconnected (human and non-human alike)." Art, in this framework, is "a *thin(g)king* space or a zone of contact where the foreign language of things breaks through to modify human perceptual grasping."[1] Thin(g)king indicates "a moment of contamination in cognitive-perceptual circuitry by the intrusion of a vibrant power that is not its own."[2]

Hood and Lewis sense these more-than-human encounters between a human artist and the items she searches for in second-hand stores to use in her projects. As the artist was called to certain materials, she "at times she made 'oohing' sounds," which were simple but "varied in pitch and length. The more energy an object emitted, the stronger the noise seemed to be, meaning the duration of the ooh would be longer, and the volume longer." In the moment of the encounter, the language is not of the human or the object, but between the two. "Neither inside nor outside of language, oohing and ahhing are transversal modes of communication."[3] These verbal expressions don't communicate determinate knowledge but vocalize the indeterminacy of the encounter of the in-between.[4] Thin(g)king provides a way to

---

1   Emily Jean Hood and Tyson E. Lewis, "'Oohing and Ahhing': The Power of Thin(g)king in Art Education Research," *International Journal of Education Through Art* 17, no. 2 (2021): 224.

2   Ibid., 229.

3   Ibid., 230.

4   These are not mutually exclusive endeavors. See Derek R. Ford, *Communist Study: Education for the Commons*, 2nd ed. (Lanham: Lexington Books, 2022), 105-117.

think about unlearning's epistemology.

This chapter fleshes out the aesthetics of thin(g)king with the work of Louis Althusser. By analyzing his writings on aesthetics and configuring them within his broader political project, I draw out the aesthetic, educational, and political function of "more-than-human" materiality. If the previous chapter developed different pedagogical logics operating in the aesthetic terrain of the class struggle, this one moves those logics to the topography of knowledge and thought, or the contrasting epistemologies operative in each educational form. Althusser provides a range of concepts as well as an extensive theoretical framework to think through the pedagogical function of aesthetics, especially how it sets us up to not only know but to *think* and *sense* the actuality of revolution.

THE PEDAGOGY OF ALTHUSSER'S POLITICS

Althusser's interventions are theoretical battles regarding explicit elements of the conjuncture. Many "critiques" of his work (especially his first few publications) miss this context and mistake his interventions for a philosophical essence or universal principle. In his reply to "The Althusser Case," a lengthy polemic from British communist John Lewis, Althusser starts by sarcastically thanking the author for the "opportunity [...] to clear up certain matters, twelve years after the event."[5] While *Marxism Today* published "The Althusser Case" in 1972, the symptoms addressed in the "case" were mainly from Althusser's book, *For Marx*, which contained articles written between 1960-1964 and appeared the following year. In the book's introduction, the only

---

5   Louis Althusser, "Reply to John Lewis," in L. Althusser, *On Ideology* (New York: Verso, 1971/2008), 65.

part written in 1965, Althusser presents the articles as historical documents representing interventions in the ideological and theoretical conjuncture in the French communist movement (particularly the French Communist Party), expressly framing them as works "marked by their date of birth, even in their inconsistencies, which I have decided not to correct."[6]

A determining element in this battle was essentialist readings of Marx, which were propelled by the then-recent dissemination of Marx's early works, published as the *Economic and Philosophic Manuscripts of 1844* (also referred to as the *Paris Manuscripts*).[7] Essentialists viewed the manuscripts—which Marx never tried to publish—as the newly found key to unlocking the entire trajectory of Marx's research. In these works, however, Marx still hadn't broken from Hegel nor, as a result, had he developed the revolutionary dialectic or, as we saw in the introduction, the method of historical materialism. Essentialists searched for *the* inherent contradiction or element in the class struggle, such as the contradiction between the productive forces and means of production (economism) or between the human and capital (humanism) that linearly drive history forward.[8] What Marx teaches instead is that "simplicity is merely the product of the complex process."[9] For example, while Marx's

---

6   Louis Althusser, *For Marx*, trans. B. Brewster (New York: Verso, 1965/2005), 21.

7   For more on one of the central themes in this debate, see Hannah Dickinson and Curry Malott, "What is Alienation? The Development and Legacy of Marx's Early Theory," *Liberation School*, 07 December 2021.

8   See David I. Backer, *The Gold and the Dross: Althusser for Educators* (Boston: Brill, 2019).

9   Althusser, *For Marx*, 196.

account of *so-called* primitive accumulation in England in *Capital* appears as the "simple" process of divorcing immediate producers from their means of subsistence and transforming the latter into capital, it's only possible to posit such a simple formulation retroactively—through the method of the "practical communist"—because multifaceted and provisional circumstances, contradictions, and encounters propel the class struggle. We can only derive general principles by abstracting away from such particularities.

In his rejection of essentialism, therefore, Althusser highlights the complexity, contingency, and heterogeneity of capitalist social formations and the class struggle. This both deepens our analysis of the various forces operating in any given conjuncture and enables our strategic and tactical decisions. I find Althusser's distinction between two different kinds of thinking or manners of practicing philosophy helpful for clarifying marxism against essentialism. The first "reflects on necessity's *fait accompli*," as it takes the existing totality as an inevitable result of the gradual unfolding of fundamental contradictions. The second, on the other hand, "reflects on the present in the present, on the necessity to be achieved, on the means to produce it, on the strategic application points for these means."[10] In other words, marxist philosophers approach the conjuncture as the actualization of past accomplishments and position revolution as something that *must* be achieved: *the actuality of revolution*.

Marxist philosophy, then, "produces not knowledge, but only a weapon in a fight."[11] Because philosophy's answers are weapons, they "cannot be called 'true,'" but only "'correct' [*juste*],

---

10   Ibid., 179.

11   Althusser, *Philosophy for Non-Philosophers*, 180.

if this adjective, *'correct'*, *designates the effect of an adjustment* that takes into account all the elements of a given situation in which a class is struggling to attain its objectives."[12] The validity of any philosophical thesis is confirmed through struggle and practice. The question is not: "is it true?" but: "does it correspond to the conjuncture in a way that advances the interests of the oppressed and exploited?" A philosophical thesis is validated not by abstract principles or proofs, but by its effect on the movement and its ideology. If philosophy produces theses for the class struggle to produce a different world, then perhaps unlearning produces *experiences* that demonstrate the reality of alternative worlds.

Unlearning transforms the raw materials of education (e.g., content and subjects) by redistributing them to produce a sensation that we can be radically different than we are now. We might say that schooling is the interpellation of the subject into the ideological framework of capitalism, and education is the *disinterpellation* of the subject *out* of capitalist ideology and into an open space.[13] Althusser defines ideology as the "imaginary relationship of individuals to their real conditions of existence."[14] The encounter of unlearning is pivotal because ideology "has very little to do with 'consciousness' [...] it is profoundly unconscious, even when it presents itself in a reflected form."[15] The imagination exists *materially* as it's reproduced through actions and practices.

---

12   Ibid., 182.

13   This term is from Tyson E. Lewis.

14   Louis Althusser, *On the Reproduction of Capitalism*, ed. J. Bidet, trans. B. Brewster and G.M. Goshgarian (New York: Verso, 1995/2014), 256.

15   Althusser, *For Marx*, 233.

The adherent to a Church isn't interpellated as a subject through learning specific content but through learning the proper bodily movements and sensations. Ideology's perceptual reproduction is enacted through varying modes: "the materialities of a displacement for going to mass, of kneeling down, of the gesture of the sign of the cross, or of the *mea culpa*, of a sentence, of a prayer, of an act of contrition, of a penitence, of a gaze, of a hand-shake, of an external verbal discourse or an 'internal' verbal discourse (consciousness)."[16] Take school, for instance. What matters for capital is not really *what* we learn in schools but *how* we learn to perform in schools. The capitalist educational system "requires not only that its *qualifications* be reproduced, but that its *submission* to the rules of respect for the established order be reproduced at the same time."[17] During the time that we learn math or art, we also learn when to sit down and when to stand up, how to follow directions, the proper way to ask questions, what to do when bells ring, how to relate to our colleagues and superiors, how our superiors relate to their superiors, and so on.[18] This is because capital has to reproduce labor-power (meaning the specific skills it requires) as well as the laborer (meaning the person in whom the labor-power is embodied).

The marxist educational scene interrupts capitalist ideology through disinterpellation, creating an unexpected and unforeseeable encounter that disorders—and divorces us from—capi-

16   Althusser, *On the Reproduction of Capitalism*, 260-261.

17   Ibid., 51.

18   The idea that the social relations of schooling square with the social relations of capital is further developed in Samuel Bowles and Herbert Gintis, *Schooling in Capitalist America: Educational Reform and the Contradictions of Economic Life* (New York: Basic Books, 1976).

tal's perceptual regime by transforming the raw materials of the conjuncture. Unlearning doesn't produce encounters but does make them possible. "Every encounter is," Althusser announces, "contingent, and necessarily contingent," which "opens up unprecedented perspectives on events, and thus also on history and time."[19] To return again to Marx's account of *so-called* primitive accumulation in England, Althusser argues that this section, "the true heart of the book" presents "the emergence of a historical phenomenon whose result we know [...] but whose causes bear no relation to the result and its effects."[20] It is not as if the myriad elements that comprise the process–from colonialism and slavery to the enclosure of the commons and the legislation against the poor–were the teleological result of an intentional process. Instead, they were various elements that encountered each other and eventually took hold to produce a new mode of production.

The encounter is aleatory, unpredictable, and potentially fleeting. There's no causal relationship between an intention and the encounter, nor is there "any line of inquiry that can trace back to its ultimate cause" because "the appearance of the swerve cannot be predicted by any agency—any trajectory leading from *a* to *z* is inherently unstable and given over to chance."[21] Unable to ensure it, the aleatory teacher nonetheless *intends* to bring about the encounter and is receptive to its surfacing. The teacher's task is to pry open and maintain "a space for an encounter by

19   Althusser, *How to be a Marxist in Philosophy*, 101.

20   Althusser, *Philosophy of the Encounter*, 199.

21   Tyson E. Lewis, "A Marxist Education of the Encounter: Althusser, Interpellation, and the Seminar," *Rethinking Marxism* 29, no. 2 (2017): 313.

setting up the possibilities for a clash" between different matter (subjects and objects).[22] The teacher *pushes* potential encounters further: "Keep going with that!" "Tell us more!" To do this, the teacher must *show* the encounter's presence by setting up the conditions for what Althusser calls "the most dramatic and difficult trial of all, the discovery of and training in the meaning of the 'simplest' acts of existence: seeing, listening, speaking, reading."[23] The teacher identifies and points to the traces of alternatives within the present, moving the collective to new territory. For me, this means that the encounter of marxist education is guided not only by knowledge but by thought. As my comrade Nino Brown put it after reading this, thought is the experience of conceptualizing how to shift tactics and strategies in response to new political developments—the educational experience of wonder—guided by the knowledge of marxist theory.

THOUGHT AND THE AESTHETICS OF CLASS STRUGGLE

In a letter to one of his colleagues, Althusser makes some partial but provocative statements about the role of art in the class struggle based on his own encounters with *particular* objects and events in determinate conjunctures. He tells him that art "does not replace knowledge (in the modern sense: scientific knowledge), but what it gives us does nevertheless maintain a certain *specific relationship* with knowledge." This is a pedagogy of unlearning in that it doesn't produce any determinate result

---

22   Ibid., 314.

23   Louis Althusser, "From *Capital* to Marx's Philosophy," in L. Althusser, É. Balibar, R. Establet, P. Macherey, and J. Rancière, *Reading Capital*, trans. B. Brewster and D. Fernbach (New York: Verso, 1965/20015), 15-16.

but rather lets us "*see*, *perceive* (but not *know*) something which *alludes* to reality."[24] Science produces *knowledge*—even if that knowledge is never fully complete and always in process—and philosophy produces *theses*. Aesthetic education, by contrast, produces the *experience* of *knowledge in the making*, or the immersion in the *disjuncture* of thought, which can be neither true nor correct, only *possible*. I would suggest, then, that in marxism, philosophy aims for correct theses, science aims for concrete knowledge, while aesthetic education aims at the experience of revolutionary possibility, or the *sensation* of the revolution to be accomplished.

Althusser's essay on Carlo Bertolazzi's play *El Nost Milan* performs the aesthetic and pedagogical capacities needed to sense the actuality of revolution and serves as an example of an intervention in the struggle to produce political art. Organized around two contradictory temporalities, each of the play's acts begin with the empty and ahistorical time of capital. In the first act, there are "a good thirty characters who come and go in this empty space, waiting for who knows what, for something to happen [...] in their lives, in which nothing happens."[25] The ideological (chronological) time of capitalism is when "the time of political events is over and done with."[26] This empty time mediates capitalist production and exchange as it's "a stationary time in which nothing resembling History can yet happen, an empty time, accepted as empty."[27] Capital's time clashes with another

---

24   Louis Althusser, *Lenin and Philosophy and Other Essays*, trans. B. Brewster (New York: Monthly Review Press, 1971/2001), 152.

25   Althusser, *For Marx*, 131-132.

26   Althusser, *How to be a Marxist in Philosophy*, 110.

27   Althusser, *For Marx*, 136.

time in the last moments of the act where, "in a flash a 'story' is sketched out, the image of destiny" as a young girl, Nina watches a clown's performance through a circus tent. "For one moment," Althusser recalls, "time is in suspense."[28] The promise of a child's wonder conflicts with the danger of the child's life, as we glimpse the town pimp eyeing Nina.

This conflict is an *interruption* that jars the scene and the ahistorical time of capital to make us *feel* the possibility of History. The lack of any relation between the ahistorical, stagnant time of capital and the abrupt, exhaustive time of History amounts to a lesson in the presence of other presents. The educational encounter generated by the rupturing event of the play's organization creates a perception of the possibility of History, which "is nothing but the permanent revocation of the accomplished fact by another undecipherable fact to be accomplished, without our knowing in advance whether, or when, or how the event that revokes it will come about."[29] We feel History's possibility by experiencing incommensurable, coexisting times through an internal distance within the play's architecture. Instead of identifying with or recognizing ourselves in the characters, the play's configuration produces a distance between our consciousness and the possibility of another kind of consciousness, teaching us by pointing to a gap.

This staging is similar to what Althusser experiences in the paintings of Leonardo Cremonini, whose works perform a marxist rendering of society. Cremonini doesn't paint concrete things, times, spaces, or events, but "'paints' the *relations* which

---

28   Ibid., 132.

29   Althusser, *Philosophy of the Encounter*, 174.

bind the objects, places and times."[30] While no one can "paint social relations" or "the relations of production or the forms of the class struggle in a given society," it *is* possible "to 'paint' visible connections that depict by their disposition the *determinate absence* which governs them."[31] We can't know the class struggle or the mode of production because we can't see the abstract relations that govern them, but we can sense these abstractions through their heterogeneity and the disjointed juxtaposition of presences and absences. This sensation evokes a shift from exchange-value to use-value, from product to process, from knowledge to thought.

Knowing involves a determinate judgment that occurs when given data comes under the mind's order and comprehension, even if that ordering is only temporary, the raw materials for another order. Thinking is, conversely, an exposure to the process of knowledge production itself, which takes place *beyond* the subject's mental powers. Thought is what fractures the ability to know in the first place. During the ahistorical time of capitalism in *El Nost Milan*, a time in which nothing really happens, we might try to understand the characters, their lives, their context, and their relations. The suspension of capital's time with Historical time, however, *interrupts* those effects, exposing us to the outside of knowledge, to our inability to know: to the experience of thought. In the play, this happens temporally; in the paintings, it happens spatially.

Why distinguish between knowledge and thought now? Capital's flexibility allows it to accommodate and profit from all manner of knowledges, even oppositional ones. If difference is

---

30   Althusser, *Lenin and Philosophy and Other Essays*, 157-158.

31   Ibid., 162.

articulated and presented as knowledge, capital can productively incorporate it, not only blunting its oppositional force but energizing capital's perceptual ecology.[32] Even communist science can be antagonistic and subjectable to capital, which is why it's significant that art *isn't* a form of scientific knowledge. As he tells his colleague, historical materialists should produce "*scientific* concepts" of art "to *know* it, and to give it its due," although by knowing it we neither "pass art silently by nor sacrifice it to science."[33] That is to say, for Althusser art becomes a political weapon through the pedagogy of unlearning. Althusser performs this aesthetic pedagogy when he ends his essay on the play by confessing, "I look back, and I am suddenly and irresistibly assailed by *the* question: are not these few pages [...] simply that unfamiliar play *El Nost Milan*, performed on a June evening, pursuing in me its incomplete meaning, searching in me, despite myself, now that all the actors and sets have been cleared away, for the *advent* of its silent discourse?"[34] The play and Althusser's commentary *present* the multiple times coexisting in the present, visible times we can measure and "invisible rhythms and punctuations concealed beneath the surface of each visible time."[35] As temporal interruptions, Althusser points us to the time that we can only think and experience: the time of revolution.

---

32   See Ford, *Communist Study*, 67-78.

33   Althusser, *Lenin and Philosophy and Other Essays*, 155.

34   Althusser, *For Marx*, 151.

35   Louis Althusser, "The Object of *Capital*," in L. Althusser, É. Balibar, R. Establet, P. Macherey, and J. Rancière, *Reading Capital*, trans. B. Brewster and D. Fernbach (New York: Verso, 1965/2015), 248.

THINKING THE EDUCATIONAL ENCOUNTER

My discussion of Cremonini overlooked a focal aspect of Althusser's experience: the paintings Althusser sees are the abstract relations "between 'men' and their 'things,' or rather, to give the term its stronger sense, between 'things' and *their* 'men.'"[36] We can now return to the "more than human materiality" at the basis of Hood and Lewis' methodology and find it immanent in the conjunctural elements of politics, aesthetics, and pedagogy. What is Althusser saying except that this aesthetic experience makes it possible to research, in the words of Hood and Lewis "the more-than-human assemblages that make up a specific context?"[37] It is neither the human nor the relations between and amongst human and other material objects that constitute the setting of such research. It is instead "*an authorless theatre*" that "is simultaneously its own stage, its own script, its own actors" and whose "spectators can, on occasion, be spectators only because they are first of all forced to be its actors, caught by the constraints of a script and parts whose authors they cannot be."[38] This visibility of the totality of capital "is as much a part of the reality of social relations as is the other appearance, that of the immediacy and transparency of the relations between men and 'their things' or 'their products.'"[39] Is not the last formulation a reiteration of what Althusser finds so revolutionary about Cremonini's paintings? Marx doesn't want to uncover the *human* labor behind things but to let us, by way of religious, literary, and economic *dramaturgy*, come to know and feel the real ab-

---

36   Althusser, *Lenin and Philosophy and Other Essays*, 158.

37   Hood and Lewis, "'Oohing and Ahhing,'" 227.

38   Althusser, "The Object of *Capital*," 349.

39   Althusser, *Philosophy of the Encounter*, 128.

stractions that govern us.

In our conjuncture, the balance of forces between the exploiters and exploited, the oppressors and oppressed, is shifting toward the latter, although the former is still dominant. The temporality of our current moment in which the class struggle is debilitated by the incredulity of the actuality of revolution (or the impossibility of History) is exactly the temporality of the chronological time in *El Nost Milan*. The claim is not that we can or should import this singular performance Althusser recounts into our own time but that his writing provides documentation and produces a sensation of the punctures that propel social movements. This aesthetic experience can be the object of marxist pedagogical practice, such as what Lewis advances, in which "something happens; some comments, gestures, discussions cause a swerve effect that cannot be predicted but that nevertheless alters the direction of the seminar." As an organizer for encounters of unlearning, the marxist teacher exposes students "to an opening for a swerve [...] bearing witness and maintaining the clash of atoms when the swerve occurs ('Go with that!')."[40] Unlearning surfaces in the aesthetic disjuncture between subjects and objects, or between humans and *their* things (like texts) or things and *their* humans.

These encounters are contingent, unplanned, and uncontrollable. Any knowledge engendered will only be retroactively assigned because the encounter is not guided by any teleology or reason—and because "simplicity is merely the product of the complex process."[41] The revolutionary teacher doesn't merely arrange for encounters: they arrange for encounters that might ad-

---

40   Lewis, "A Marxist Education of the Encounter," 316.

41   Althusser, *For Marx*, 196.

vance the class struggle. Introducing "more-than-human" matter into aesthetic education marks another fundamental aspect of our current conjuncture: our conception of subjectivity and materiality. The aesthetics of marxist pedagogy entail a "thin(g) king [...] that is not bound up in a singular material body, but rather happens through the comingling of material bodies."[42] The pedagogy of the authorless theater is significant in this regard, as it demonstrates the suppressed reality and possibility of collectivity against the abstraction of the individually-bounded thing that holds the class struggle back.

The pedagogical and political materiality of aesthetics "allows the audience not simply to 'suspend its disbelief' but to do so willingly."[43] The spectator and the actor are, similarly, nothing but the effects of the vibrant relations of the forces operative in the conjuncture. The authorless theater engages pedagogy as the complex interplay of forces under determinate historical conditions. We act as determined subjects within the conjuncture that in turn determines the distribution and perceptual configuration of these energies. Together, we compose the authorless theater of ideology "because a given work originally 'belongs' to no one, it can be assigned to anyone."[44] No matter how comprehensive and total capital's perceptual ecology appears, there is always a void we can occupy. These political encounters teach the actuality of revolution by decomposing individuality and facilitating our disidentification with capital.

---

42   Hood and Lewis, "'Oohing and Ahhing,'" 229.

43   Warren Montag, "Althusser's Authorless Theater," *differences* 26, no. 3 (2015): 45.

44   Ibid., 44.

CHAPTER 4

LISTENING FOR WHAT WE DON'T KNOW

In a short manuscript posthumously published as *What is to be Done?* Althusser obliquely addresses the relationship between theoretical knowledge and the encounter. He starts by stressing that the political question of orienting and organizing the class struggle upholds "the primacy of the political line over the party, and the construction and organization of the party *as a function* of the political line."[1] Both the organization and the line it's built on articulate the contemporary conjuncture of the class struggle, and Althusser identifies two raw materials the party assembles to determine the conjunctural analysis. The first are produced by petitioning workers "to talk about their lives, their jobs, how they are exploited, and the like," through means such as letters to the editor. Going to "the field, without preparation, and interview[ing] the workers" generates the second raw material. Both raw materials are necessary but insufficient for grasp-

---

1   Althusser, *What is to be Done?*, 1.

ing the current conjuncture and for "*preparing* for this encounter."[2] The two materials are *articulated* and involve speaking and listening, the latter of which is incomplete without the third raw material: theoretical and political knowledge. Their insufficiency stems from their one-sidedness in that they only entail relations between individual workers and not an encounter with the totality of the complex class antagonism in its current state, remaining only *elements* instead of *relations of force*.

To prepare for the political encounter and to better sense the complexity of the conjuncture, party members must gain "the ability to '*listen correctly*' [...] when face-to-face with workers talking about their life and work." Listening correctly is defined by the listeners' capability 1) to "know which questions to ask and which not to;" 2) "to put what the workers say into relation with what the workers themselves do not know about the effects that the general process has on their own condition;" and 3) to *listen for what they don't know*, or to "be open to learning, by way of this relation, what they do not know and what the workers do, but without knowing that they know it.[3] Proper listening consists in prompting the right line of investigation, placing the response within theoretical and political knowledge of the totality, and finally, listening for what the worker knows without knowing it and what the inquirer doesn't know. This last competence is somewhat confounding. How, after all, can one listen for what one doesn't know or for what the *sound doesn't say*? Even more fundamentally, how does one prepare for the encounter by acquiring the ability to listen for what we can't know or hear?

---

2   Ibid., 3.

3   Ibid., 12.

Althusser repeatedly gestures to the inaudible dimensions of the class struggle throughout his works. In his essay on the encounter, for example, he writes that "silence is a *political* condition for the encounter."[4] More relevant to this project, in *On the Reproduction of Capitalism*, Althusser listens to the silence of capitalist ideology and education. He conceptualizes Ideological State Apparatuses as a concert "dominated by a single score [...] the score of the ideology of the current ruling class." In the score, "one Ideological State Apparatus certainly has the dominant role, although hardly anyone lends an ear to its music: it is so silent! This is the school."[5] To sense the silent score of capitalist ideology and the silent condition of the encounter, we listen for what we can't hear, for the inaudible. This chapter pursues this latent but persistent aesthetic and pedagogical problematic so we might retrain ourselves in this "simplest" act of existence by unlearning it.

THE MUSIC OF CAPITAL

Some recent works on the political economy of music and sound provide entry points for thinking about the sonic dimensions of the perceptual ecology of capital and the actuality of revolution. In *Music and Capitalism*, Timothy Taylor takes up not the *effects* of capitalism on music but the *causes* of those effects. Because most of what we consider music today would be impossible without capitalism (as it's produced, distributed, and consumed as a commodity), this area needs attention.[6] The real

---

4   Althusser, *Philosophy of the Encounter*, 172.

5   Althusser, *On the Reproduction of Capitalism*, 251.

6   Timothy D. Taylor, *Music and Capitalism: A History of the Present* (Chicago: The University of Chicago Press, 2017), 24-25.

issue isn't whether or to what extent music's been commodified, but in what value regimes it's produced and circulated. Music, like any "cultural" product, is not special or unique but is, simply, a commodity. Still, as a commodity it has a use-value, which is singular and heterogeneous, historical and contingent, traversing limits in space and time, exceeding the boundaries of any region and any individual life.

Without reliable funding and state support, musicians today adapt to a flexible market by, for instance, becoming public figures, taking jobs in art criticism, or writing memoirs. The thesis of art's autonomy again justifies this shift so that, "to this day, the idea that the artist and her work somehow stand apart from society remains strong."[7] Throughout the 20th century, musical production and distribution made radical twists and turns through new recording devices and playback machines, greater accessibility to recording studios and equipment, and so on. Capital also found a new source of value in counterculture in the 1950s, something from which the record industry was able to profit, which allowed it to "internalize" the artistic critique of capitalism and channel resistance into the individual subject-form and frame liberation through the commodity-form.

Taylor maps the commodification of musical labor and the changing working conditions and organizations of production and distribution because music forms "what people think and feel and should play a potent role in promoting ideologies of how the world is."[8] Nonetheless, music can and does exist outside of capitalist relations and he finds hope in restricted fields of production where people make music for others. This opens

---

7   Ibid., 32.

8   Ibid., 13.

a space for minority cultures that represent "one way to attempt to escape the ever-expanding net of today's capitalism" insofar as musicians in these fields are "aloof from" or ignorant of the profit motive.[9] Even though capital can and does capture such subfields, the fact they continue to proliferate signals a collective desire to produce an alternative musical world.

Marianna Ritchey examines the contradictory effects of classical music in neoliberalism and how the ideas of the latter filter through the former while the former reinforces and naturalizes the latter. She focuses on digital technologies and tech companies because they're the vanguard of neoliberalism and because they fetishize innovation and creativity. But here's the rub: "Tech firms present the past as a nightmare from which their products deliver us via ceaseless innovation; yet this relentlessly progressive vision does not gibe with the very notion of *the classic*, a term that since the late eighteenth century has been used to indicate objects whose value is perceived as eternal and unchanging."[10] As classical music is thought to be in decline, it needs innovation and democratization. It needs to be accessible, to speak to the masses; it thereby needs to be disrupted, innovated, and remixed with digital technologies and post-Fordist labor practices. This emerges in music education through "the necessity to 'innovate' classical music by enlivening it with technology of various kinds," "new modes of musician training that will encourage young artists to become flexible, adaptable, and self-managing individuals" working to extend classical music beyond the orchestra halls by making "music easier for untrained

---

9   Ibid., 170.

10   Marianna Ritchey, *Composing Capital: Classical Music in the Neoliberal Era* (Chicago: The University of Chicago Press, 2019), 2.

listeners to consume."[11]

The ideology of art's autonomy is vital for *capital* because, as music's autonomy is a fact established through political struggles, the positioning of classical music as a truly autonomous art form allows corporations to "use historical ideas and stereotypes of classical music" to "help these corporations appear virtuous to the populations they plunder."[12] Because classical music represents one of the primary examples of musical autonomy, when mobilized by corporations, compositions like Beethoven's "convey the impression of sublime, timeless truth." The alleged autonomy of classical music functions as "a soothing pacifier for neoliberal marketers to use on citizens" because of classical music's "obvious associations with *the classic*, a term that began being used in the eighteenth century to indicate timeless moral virtue."[13] Capitalist firms use classical music's autonomy to link their products with timeless and ahistorical values. At the same time, Ritchey highlights the *ambivalence* of art's autonomy. The potentially radical side of the art autonomy thesis, which she concludes the book with, is "the chipping away of even the *desire* for a noncommodified space."[14]

More recently, Ritchey seeks to recover and redeploy art's autonomy against contemporary capital. In this framework, "art that is abstract, that lacks a participatory ethos, that fetishizes perfection, technique, and training, or that is otherwise seen as inaccessible to the masses [...] becomes effectively useless."[15]

11   Ibid., 4.

12   Ibid., 2.

13   Ibid., 123.

14   Ibid., 161.

15   Marianna Ritchey, "Resisting Usefulness: Music and the Politi-

Ritchey conceives of a *collective* artistic autonomy that "must be explicitly anticapitalist" and "able to encompass a vast array of difference in terms of how to make, hear, and know about music."[16] The inability to *know* music is present in *Composing Capital*, where Ritchey salvages the important function of music's incomprehensibility, arguing that its opacity "can cause us to question what we think we know, and why and how we know it: What is 'music,' and why do I think it ought to sound a certain way? Who told me that music ought to sound in such a way, and why?"[17] Here, the inaccessibility of music generates the thoughtful contemplation and imagination required for revolutionary politics. Elsewhere, art for art's sake represents the desire for *life* rather than *a job* and is linked with music's ephemerality, which prevents its total capture by capital.

Ritchey's agnosticism towards the reality of art's autonomy is constructive in that she's not interested in affirming or denying its correspondence with reality but in exploring *why* it's been so appealing across such diverse periods and broad stretches of place. And, most importantly, Ritchey acknowledges that neither music nor critique substitute for political action and organization. Taylor's account of capital's flexible accumulation strategies foregrounds the danger of assigning music or any "cultural" commodity a privileged position in reproducing or resisting capitalism. By drawing out the historical production of music under capitalism they both explain how capital structures the organization of audibility and foreground our attempts to escape that structure by producing a non-capitalist sonic sur-

cal Imagination," *Current Musicology* 108 (2021): 34.

16   Ibid., 48-49.

17   Ritchey, *Composing Capital*, 151.

round without either consigning those attempts to inevitable incorporation into capital or valorizing them as surefire paths of resistance.

Symptomatic Listening

If music as a sensuous object opens a space for a counterhegemonic imaginary, then we have to attend to *listening* practices and how we unlearn to sense music and sound in general. What kind of education do we need in what kind of aesthetics to unlearn capitalist imperialism and open ourselves up to encounters with others? Such listening is surely that which Althusser is after, a stupid listening for sounds that we don't know how to hear and that don't know how to speak to us, enabling an exposure to a silence that makes the encounter possible politically. I find a model of the final kind of listening Althusser urges his comrades to do in the writing and reading he practiced in *Reading Capital*, both of which were less sonic than they were visual or, put better, were visual practices of audibility.[18]

His pedagogy here implies that knowledge can't be produced by listening to "manifest discourse, because the text of history is not a text in which a voice (the Logos) speaks, but the inaudible and illegible notation of the effects of a structure of structures."[19] Immediately, Althusser is clear that the inaudibility of the text is not metaphorical, but literal. The invisible isn't the *outside* of the visible, which would only necessitate an immediate reading of the unread. Instead, "the invisible is defined by the visible as *its* invisible, *its* forbidden vision: the invis-

---

18   Derek R. Ford, *Inhuman Educations: Jean-François Lyotard, Pedagogy, Thought* (Boston: Brill, 2021), 44-54.

19   Althusser, "From *Capital* to Marx's Philosophy," 15.

ible is not therefore simply what is outside the visible."[20] Marxist reading is like scientific production, which "*lives*, by the extreme attention it pays to the points where it is theoretically fragile." For the marxist reader—and listener—silence isn't merely what is excluded from the text "but *par excellence* what it contains that is fragile despite its apparently unquestionable 'obviousness', certain silences in its discourse" or, "in brief, everything in it that 'sounds hollow' to an attentive ear, despite its fullness."[21] Such marxist (or symptomatic) reading, "is attuned to the opacity of the object and the conceits of the concept."[22] Listening symptomatically is both philosophical and aesthetic, producing infinite theses to test, each test an aesthetic experience of the materiality of thought and a political attempt to test a philosophical hypothesis.

Althusser posits symptomatic reading just after he pleads with us to reinvent the "simplest" ways of sensing. This reading is far from that of the "master" who commands his students to follow his path and whose "theory of education is committed to preserving the power it seeks to bring to light."[23] Rancière critiques his former teacher's written pedagogy, arguing that Althusser's texts operate according to the logic of an elementary school textbook.[24] The dotted lines in such textbooks represent words that the teacher knows and that the student must

---

20   Ibid., 25.

21   Ibid., 29.

22   Robyn Marasco, "Althusser's Gramscian Debt: On Reading Out Loud," *Rethinking Marxism* 31, no. 3 (2019): 343.

23   Rancière, *Althusser's Lesson*, 52.

24   Jacques Rancière, *The Flesh of Words: The Politics of Writing*, trans. C. Mandell (Stanford: Stanford University Press, 1998/2004).

accurately discern. Althusser *knows* how to speak the silences because the dots are only the absent presence of the master himself. As Lewis astutely notes, however, these critiques contradict Rancière's actual descriptions of Althusser's classroom pedagogy, which convey that Althusser, in fact, "says very little (i.e. there is silence instead of speech), and the students are left to construct the answers for themselves."[25] Althusser's lesson repositions the pedagogical gesture from the cognitive to the aesthetic.

Althusser's marxist reading is irreducible to either the acquisition or the production of new knowledges because it "opens up the possibility of a fissure between sense (the common sense of the subject) and sense (as the sensation of difference beyond the sensory perception of the subject."[26] Althusser merely tries to listen for the silences and to teach us to listen, too. *This* is the knowledge the teacher must *teach* to the student. The pedagogical problematic in *Reading Capital* is not that of the expert or master theoretician imparting the truth to others, but "is first and foremost a pedagogy of affective rupture and redistribution" where "reading cannot be reduced to the mere cognitive acquisition of the various complexities of *Capital*."[27] Colin Davis verifies that Althusser's "symptomatic reading ensures that meaning is produced, in process, but never stable or unitary" and that "misunderstanding and misrecognition belong to the process as much as or more than their opposites."[28] There is no *final transparency* and no *final audible articulation* of any eternal

---

25   Lewis, *The Aesthetics of Education*, 24.

26   Ibid., 30.

27   Ibid., 29.

28   Colin Davis, "Althusser on Reading and Self-Reading," *Textual Practice* 15, no. 2 (2001): 304.

"truth" because marxist reading produces another abyss within the discourse and the fields of sight and sound.

Because the test is always to be taken, Althusser's primary beef with idealist philosophers is their self-positioning as "one who knows that others don't; and who also knows what the true meaning of what others know is [...] who, in a certain way, claims to possess, from the very beginning, the truth's birth certificate."[29] They start from the absolute beginning of the problem to pursue it and arrive at its solution. Althusser repeatedly uses the imagery of the philosopher and the train. Idealist philosophers hop on the train at the original, departing station and ride it until it reaches its end. Idealist philosophy is, as such, *teleological*, in that it is "an oriented process, a goal-directed [...] process." Materialist philosophers, on the contrary, "always board a moving train."[30] We begin where we are, denounce even the possibility of identifying an absolute origin, and don't profess to produce any truth.

Given this, it's surprising that Rancière frames Althusser's textual pedagogy as dotted lines of an elementary school textbook. In this model, the student proves their knowledge to the master by correctly filling in the absences left by the master. Lewis provides a better framing that models his teaching as falling dots of rain, like those Althusser uses to open his short treatise on the materialism of the encounter. "It is raining," he writes. "Let this book therefore be, before all else, a book about ordinary rain."[31] The rain represents how the world—and History—emerges. Before the world, "an infinity of atoms were falling parallel to

---

29   Althusser, *How to be a Marxist in Philosophy*, 146.

30   Ibid., 18.

31   Althusser, *Philosophy of the Encounter*, 167.

each other" until something made one "swerve" into another, producing "*an encounter* with the atom next to it, and, from encounter to encounter, a pile-up and the birth of a world."[32] To translate this into the language of the previous chapter, before History happens innumerable contradictions occur in a social formation until for some contingent reason one swerves into another, and still another, and a revolutionary rupture occurs and a new mode of production takes hold.

Ordered developmentally according to the logic of learning, the textbook dots are "uniformly wedded to the page by a particular subject."[33] Arranged to facilitate encounters according to the logic of unlearning, the dots take the form of silences the teacher or author can't or won't determine. In the end, then, Rancière mistakes Althusser's silence as an *origin* instead of as a *beginning*. As an origin, silence awaits the teacher's answer, while as a beginning, silence remains open to the encounter.

Listening for What We Can't Hear

Althusser's pedagogy points to a silence beyond the current field of audibility. One place he points to this silence is in his reading of Machiavelli's *The Prince*. Machiavelli had to theorize the political necessity of establishing a national unity (Italy) simultaneously with the pedagogical necessity of creating a new political figure that could establish that project. Yet Machiavelli only points to the void from which such a struggle could begin, like the marxist educator setting up the space for the encounter. The central theoretical axiom Althusser finds in Machiavelli's theory in *The Prince* comes at the moment when

---

32   Ibid., 168, 169.

33   Lewis, *The Aesthetics of Education*, 32.

"politics appears in person," when Machiavelli addresses *what* subjective forces will accomplish the future project. While he is very explicit about the concrete nature of the book's conjuncture, Machiavelli doesn't define these forces ahead of time and instead "leaves the names of the protagonists in this encounter completely blank."[34] No one can know ahead of time precisely what composition of classes and political groupings will accomplish the revolution, only through the *political process* can and does that happen. Symptomatic listening makes sense as a sonic pedagogical form in teaching the actuality of revolution precisely because it points to the silences to be filled, demonstrating the open potential of filling those silences.

The ellipsis serves as another model where the dots on a page represent an opening to symptomatic listening. What is an ellipsis other than a present absence—or, what I'll term in the next chapter, an arrhythmic interruption—within a text? As a limit and opening, the origins of the word "ellipsis" come from the Greek words *akólouthos* and *an*, which taken together mean *not following*. The ellipsis interrupts or defers the meaning or end of a sentence, keeping thought going without annihilating the knowledge articulated. For example, when a list ends in an ellipsis, it keeps the contents of the list open to new additions and simultaneously keeps us thinking about the relationships between the content listed. In Octavia Butler's novel, *Fledgling*, the ellipsis serves as a pedagogical invitation to unlearning. Therí Alyce Pickens posits that *Fledgling* doesn't permit "the linear progressive understanding of time and narration but rather endorses the multiplicity courted by folds and gaps," bends and breaches that are the product of the overdetermination of contradictions at

---

34 Althusser, *Machiavelli and Us*, 76.

any given point in time. Reading drafts for the novel, Pickens affirms that "Butler includes ellipses not as placeholders but as parts of the dialogue and narration" that "do the work of creating silence and pausing within the narrative."[35] The breaks in the text are not moments of internal reflection or dialogue but of silences that foil any hope of accessing the author's inner life. This is muteness as a threshold of possibility that the teacher can either develop into articulation or hold open as a space for an encounter with the infinite potentiality of the present.

Listening for what we don't know, for what a sound doesn't say, is a negative pedagogical form in that it only appears as an absence or at a limit. Beyond listening as a practice, then, the sonic is a clarifying media through which to theorize. Theory is dominated by visual metaphors and processes where presence is established through a structural distance between the viewer and viewed. The sonic enables us to think *from within* a structure as it "places us inside an event" because "sounds come to" and immerse us.[36] While seeing captures and fixes, listening prevents both because sound is, by definition, movement. Sounds are errant, always disbursing from their sources outward such that we can only listen for what we can't quite hear. Along these lines, Stephen Kennedy formulates listening as that which *takes seriously* "the noise of what cannot quite be grasped or understood."[37] Unlike hearing, listening here isn't motivated by a desire to know, discover, internalize, or accumulate because it

---

35   Therí Alyce Pickens, *Black Madness :: Mad Blackness* (Durham: Duke University Press, 2019), 45.

36   Stephen Kennedy, *Future Sounds: The Temporality of Noise* (London: Bloomsbury, 2018), 132, 131.

37   Ibid., 9.

"challenge[s] our ability to make sense of the world according to a taxonomic order which organizes knowledge into discrete units, categories and disciplines."[38] Sounds, even when captured through recordings, are unlocalizable and fleeting.

While hearing is a kind of listening, it is only one kind. The differences between listening and hearing bear pedagogical and political import.[39] "If 'to hear' is to understand the sense," as Jean-Luc Nancy frames it, "to listen is to be straining toward a possible meaning, and consequently one that is not immediately accessible."[40] Hearing takes place where there is an immediate bridge between sound and meaning while listening occurs when and where there is a chasm between the two. There's no *lineari-ty* or chronological progression with listening, whereas hearing follows "a certain kind of logic that is determined to bring the universe into some kind of order, to fix it as a knowable space that proceeds through time towards definable and predictable ends."[41] This is akin to "hungry listening," Dylan Robinson's term for colonial listening, when "the listener orients teleologically toward progression and resolution, just as hunger drives toward satiation."[42] The particular form of listening I'm sounding out, by way of contrast, is an immersion in something that's only thinkable, not understandable. Listening for the thinkable pro-

---

38   Ibid., 148.

39   See Ford, *Encountering Education*, 68-85.

40   Jean-Luc Nancy, *Listening*, trans. C. Mandell (New York: Fordham University Press, 2007), 6.

41   Kennedy, *Future Sounds*, 133-134.

42   Dylan Robinson, *Hungry Listening: Resonant Theory for Indigenous Sound Studies* (Minneapolis: University of Minnesota Press, 2020), 50.

pels Althusser's directions to train Party members how to *listen* for what neither we nor other members of our class know.

Hearing, or listening to hear what we do or can know, is the sonic form of learning. Hearing is driven by the need to self-accumulate, to possess more information and knowledge, to ultimately *improve* the efficiency and performance of hearing, to better distinguish between noise and sound. Symptomatic listening is the paradoxical sonic form of unlearning. It's listening not to know but to sense the complex combinations of temporality that make the actuality of revolution perceptible. Educationally, the third form of listening Althusser calls for is important because it reasserts the pedagogical principle and ethos of acknowledging the limits to our knowledge of ourselves, our students, or our teachers. Sometimes, the more we know about our students the less open our conceptions of and approaches to them become. Althusser, moreover, asks us to recognize the limits of our self-knowledge so that we, too, can approach ourselves and the educational encounter in different ways, challenging our field of audibility—or the sounds we learn to hear and listen for through capitalist education—by listening to our listening.

LISTENING TO CAPITAL

Marx makes audible the invisible social relations that govern society under capitalism through his work on the fetishism of the commodity. Recalling our previous discussion, the reason Marx takes us from capitalism to feudalism and parochialism and then communism is "to see clearly in them what our own society hides from us." What is hidden is not the *reality* of social relations *behind* or *beneath* object relations; instead, it is the economic system itself that "is *never clearly visible*," that "does not coincide with the 'given' in them any more than in any other reality."[43] If the section on commodity fetishism were an empirical argument or phenomenological proof uncovering the hidden essence of a pre-existing form, then the concept would not be so easy to get. Out of the many difficult parts of *Capital*, this section *is* relatively easy to understand. By pointing to the commodity fetish, Marx acknowledges that, yes, when we exchange our wages for commodities, we're interacting with the international working class by participating in the social character of production. I've never had a hard time explaining this to anyone.

With Marx's concept of (surplus-)value, we can conceive the mode of production and sense the global social relations at the heart of commodity exchange. There is no "essence" that is internal to capital, nor is there anything "insubstantial" that is external to it, no anthropological reality Marx points to behind the curtain of an extraneous ideological system. Marx instead points to the invisible within the visible, rearranging our aesthetic sensibilities and teaching us to listen for the silence that's the political condition for the possibility of the communist revolution, silences like those Marx hears in capital's account of its own origins.

Guided by the pedagogy of unlearning, the teacher's gesture of pointing attends to the silences of the marginal. It's perverse to point to something that is not sensed through sight even though the act of pointing in teaching can—and most often does—entail a vocalization accompanying the gesture. Pointing to silence is necessarily going to miss its mark, as the sound is always *now* in a way that escapes the pointing and listening. All the same,

---

43   Althusser, "The Object of *Capital*," 334.

it is a mistake to conclude from this that decentering and embracing unpredictability and contingency are revolutionary in themselves, for these can be sources of accumulation and new nodes in capital's perceptual ecology—unless we acknowledge the different roles they play in pedagogy and politics.

CHAPTER 5

THE PEDAGOGY OF ARRHYTHMIA

In his conversation on literary history, Althusser takes art criticism's acceptance of a transcendental artistic essence to task by calling our attention to the pulses of history. The illusion of art as a universally and ahistorically discrete category is illuminated by art history's "basic structure of the narrative [...] that of chronology, with specific rhythms, obviously, which can simply be the rhythm of the successive years or months or the rhythm of the major events in the life of the fellow telling the story." In either instance, the analysis produces "a time about which one presupposes that it is a continuous time, the time of chronology."[1] To receive and produce an aesthetic object as an artwork that allows for different understandings while still being grouped under "art" requires a conception of history that allows for the possibility of a universal and timeless "aesthetic contact."[2] The art critic and the continuing circulation of their

1   Althusser, *History and Imperialism*, 2.
2   Ibid., 22.

object of criticism are both organized around "the same rhythm of development."[3] This is history as the repetition of similar themes building developmentally and linearly across various social formations, a sense of time that represses the actuality of revolution. Althusser doesn't go any further, but it's a historical narrative predicated on—and reproductive of—the domination of capital's abstract rhythms of production and circulation. It's here, where the pedagogical rhythms of capital and class struggle, the theoretical elaboration of the spatial and temporal aspects of the communist project come into play, that I turn to Henri Lefebvre.

After a few chapters on Althusser, the move to Lefebvre might seem odd, as the two are typically pitted against each other. Lefebvre was a "marxist humanist" while Althusser purged marxism of humanism. Lefebvre was more of an anarcho-syndicalist who left the Communist Party after a brief stint while Althusser was a longtime member. There are nonetheless good reasons to think them together in dynamic ways. Not only do both share some common concerns and even concepts but bringing in Lefebvre's theory of rhythmanalysis gives us a framework for thinking about the aesthetics of political struggle together with the times and spaces required for teaching the actuality of revolution.

Lefebvre is mostly known in the English-speaking world for his analysis of the capitalist production of space and the accompanying proposals for resisting capitalism through the cultivation of differential spaces (like the "right to the city"). His inquiry into space couldn't get far without grappling with time, and he ultimately concludes his most (and most unusually) coherent

---

3   Ibid., 4.

analysis of space, *The Production of Space*, arguing that the analysis of and struggle against capitalism require "rhythmanalysis." Not only are the spatial coordinates of the class struggle sonic; their production and transformation are educational, for rhythmanalysis, he writes, is "closer to a pedagogy of appropriation (the appropriation of the body, as of spatial practice)."[4] Here, Lefebvre introduces a conceptual pairing that preoccupies him later in *Rhythmanalysis*, another posthumously published book: linear and cyclical repetitions.

Lefebvre teaches us how and why space became centrally important in capitalism's development. "The capitalist process of production taken as a whole represents," as Marx summarizes, "a synthesis of the processes of production and circulation."[5] Space increasingly serves both functions: it's "a *product* to be used, to be consumed" as well as "a *means of production*."[6] When space serves as a mechanism for both the production and realization of capital, concrete—or what Lefebvre calls "differential"— spaces are abstracted as capital reorganizes space to facilitate the production and circulation of value. The capitalist production of space "tends to confine time to productive labour time, and simultaneously to diminish living rhythms by defining them in terms of the rationalized and localized gestures of divided labor."[7] We can overcome capitalist abstraction and domination through the analysis of existing rhythms and the generation of new, lived ones.

---

4   Henri Lefebvre, *The Production of Space*, trans. D. Nicholson-Smith (Malden: Blackwell, 1974/1991), 205.

5   Marx, *Capital (Vol. 3)*, 25.

6   Lefebvre, *The Production of Space*, 85.

7   Ibid., 408.

In *Rhythmanalysis*, Lefebvre takes up the distinction be-tween linear and cyclical repetitions and their relationship to capitalism and resistance. Rhythm involves repetition, for there is no rhythm "without *reprises*, without returns, in short with-out measure."[8] Linear and cyclical repetitions have divergent rhythms, which hinge between exchange-value and use-value. Linear rhythms, which dominate under capitalism, are "mod-elled on abstract, quantitative time, the time of watches and clocks," a "homogenous and desacralised time" determining "*the measure of the time of work*."[9] Linear rhythms are developmen-tal and repetitive, following predictable patterns in a calculating organization.

While linear repetitions, in Wozniak's words, "delimit be-coming by imposing programmed rhythms" that "aim at specific ends, particularly those of capitalist production and accumula-tion," cyclical repetitions are "open to eternal becoming" and "have a determined period or frequency that repeats itself dif-ferentially."[10] As "movements, undulations, vibrations, returns and rotations," cyclical repetitions are defined by lived concrete realities.[11] Cyclical repetitions align with what Lefebvre wanted space, time, and life to be: *differential*. Like use-value and ex-change-value, capitalist linear and cyclical repetitions can co-ex-ist in the same rhythmic assemblage, and Lefebvre isn't so much

---

8   Henri Lefebvre, *Rhythmanalysis: Space, Time and Everyday Life*, trans. S. Elden and G. Moore (London: Bloomsbury, 1992/2013), 16.

9   Ibid., 82.

10   Jason Wozniak, "Towards a Rhythmanalysis of Debt Dressage: Education as Rhythmic Resistance in Everyday Indebted Life," *Policy Futures in Education* 15, no. 4 (2017): 499.

11   Lefebvre, *Rhythmanalysis*, 84.

opposed to the former as he is to the subjection of all rhythms to the clock time of capital.

Détournement and the Rhythms of Unlearning

Because the domination of linear repetitions is political and educational, Lefebvre called his theory of rhythmanalysis a pedagogy. Part of our inauguration into the perceptual ecology of capital takes place through pedagogically structuring the rhythms of work and life. This is clear when we consider two vastly different formal educational settings. In North American Indian boarding (or residential) schools, Robinson reports, "the regimentation of activity [...] was instituted through the use of bells to organize daily activity."[12] Testimonies of boarding-school survivors express the domination of linear repetitions to the exclusion of cyclical ones. Second, in his ethnographic study in a Catholic school in Toronto, McLaren observes the imposition of "monochromatic" time as young people are forced into "the student state through a highly ritualized and institutionalized punishment and reward system" inaugurated by the teacher's statement, "You heard the bell."[13] That the pedagogical command to adhere to linear repetitions appears so clearly in remarkably disparate settings, I hope, illustrates the educational rhythmic dimension of capital's aesthetic political pedagogy and why we need to develop alternative ones.

The anti-capitalist revolution is impossible without first understanding and then intervening in the capitalist domination

---

12   Robinson, *Hungry Listening*, 56.

13   Peter McLaren, *Schooling as Ritual Performance: Toward a Political Economy of Educational Symbols and Gestures*, 3rd ed. (Lanham: Rowman & Littlefield, 1986/1999), 91.

of space and time to *appropriate* them for the working and oppressed classes. In his posthumously published work, *Towards
an Architecture of Enjoyment*, Lefebvre positions détournement
as the mediating factor between domination (exchange-value)
and appropriation (use-value). Détournement, which translates into English as "hijacking" or "repurposing," begins with
modern art, first painting and then musicking, when "musicians began mixing themes borrowed from popular song or
other musical works into their compositions, themes detached
from their content and diverted from their original meaning."[14]
Through "the moment of détournement, new aspirations appear" and what already exists is made open to new uses.[15] At the
same time, détournement is a *mediating* moment "when domination ceases," providing an opportunity for the reclamation of
space. Détournement produces "the threshold, the break, the
caesura" between either "contemplation and the dream" or "the
harsh law of profit."[16] The practice is ephemeral and can lead to
a new form of domination *or* "a more refined appropriation."[17]
Détournement is a pedagogical and political *opening* for the
conditions for appropriation. Détournement is—or was, in Lefebvre's conjuncture—a pedagogical exposure to the excessive
surplus of the contemporary aesthetic order and an experience
in another aesthetics.

Before examining the status of linear and cyclical repetitions in our era, I want to flesh out the educational modalities of

14   Henri Lefebvre, *Towards an Architecture of Enjoyment*, trans. R.
Bononno (Minneapolis: University of Minnesota Press, 2014), 96.

15   Ibid., 98.

16   Ibid., 153.

17   Ibid., 98.

rhythmanalysis through Lefebvre's triad of domination-détournement-appropriation. Cyclical repetitions remain open to détournement and maybe even appropriations. Cyclical repetition and difference are threats to capital in this model because they prioritize use-value over exchange-value and mitigate against capital's real abstraction through linear repetition. These antagonistic tempos each operate according to distinct pedagogies, or educational logics.

Learning is the pedagogical pulse of linear repetitions. The flow of learning proceeds from a state of ignorance to one of competence or mastery. The learning process begins with an inability, proceeds by measuring, assessing, and developing that inability, and results in the actualization of that ability. The trajectory takes place through the domination of bureaucratic linear temporalities over the educational and political landscape, something evident even in Freire's model of progressive decoding. In this way, learning homogenizes the complex temporalities of a given social formation, abstracting the plural times of our lives. Think about the credit-debit relation in education. As students are increasingly saddled with educational debt, we're constantly following in its wake, rendered commensurable with each other through money's abstraction. Capital imposes the pedagogy of learning through the force of debt, which is one way in which domination prevents détournement and appropriation. With the force of linear repetitions, capital abstracts space and time, reproduces the *urgentism* of the present, and represses the actuality of revolution.

Unlearning is the pedagogical pulse of cyclical repetitions. Whereas learning hinges on the linear movement from ignorance to knowledge, unlearning is a state of encountering in which we're in-between who we were and who we are, resistant to capital's quantification and measurement. By upending the demand for realization, unlearning opens the possibilities of what *can* be. The unlearner is neither ignorant nor knowledgeable, neither a novice nor a master, but a subject that rhythmically sways poetically, that "is simultaneously projective and recursive, a suspension of movement *and* its resumption, a continual oscillation of forward and backward momentum."[18] While learning's repetitions alternate between possibility and action, unlearning's rhythms are punctuated by interruptions that suspend the subject.

The learner begins developing toward a goal but becomes an unlearner by delaying any end (e.g., a second reading that leads to a third). The learner is required to pay their debts on time and produce determinate knowledge, but the unlearner always defaults, remaining in a state of potentiality. This is not passive inactivity because of its ceaseless rhythmic sway, ceaseless because of the constant deferral of any endpoint (determinant, expert knowledge; repayment of debt). Détournement, by interrupting the associations between the potential and the actual, can provoke unlearning the perceptual and rhythmic economy of capital by opening up the possibilities of what can be sensed.

CAPITAL'S CAPTURE OF CYCLICAL REPETITIONS

With this in mind, we can better excavate the educational objective and epistemology of rhythmanalysis. For Lefebvre, the *product* of rhythmanalysis surpasses philosophy and discourse to produce a "theoretical thinking" that is *even more* productive of knowledge: "To say that such theoretical thinking goes 'beyond

---

18   Lewis, *Inoperative Learning*, 27.

discourse' means that it takes account [...] of the vast store of non-formal knowledge embedded in poetry, dance, and theatre. This store of non-formal knowledge (*non-savoir*) constitutes a potential true knowledge (*connaissance*)."[19] "The joy of knowing grows desiccated," as he puts it elsewhere, "once knowledge is defined and taught and becomes an institution."[20] Opposed to this, rhythmanalysis produces "the joy of pure knowledge," which "is as short-lived as the impure pleasure of power; it wants to endure, to preserve in being, to renew itself. But to do so it requires new acts, new conquests, without end."[21] He even defines the knowledge rhythmanalysis makes as "a form of qualitative knowledge still in a state of germination and promise."[22] While this seems to be akin to unlearning, the ultimate purpose of rhythmanalysis is to acquire greater and more precise knowledge of the polyrhythms of capital to engage in constant creative production. "The authorities," according to Lefebvre, "have to know the polyrhythmia of the social body they set in motion."[23] We should, then, create and mobilize lived and differential knowledge of rhythms, which Lefebvre recommends we do by recording rhythms and then studying and reflecting on them.

In its contemporary ecology, however, capital finds profitability precisely in the openness of cyclical repetition *and* the determinations of linear repetition, which implies a new relationship between both. Maybe this is why Lefebvre's final book on rhythmanalysis follows from his move away from the city as

19   Lefebvre, *The Production of Space*, 407.

20   Lefebvre, *Towards an Architecture of Enjoyment*, 26.

21   Ibid.

22   Ibid., 149.

23   Lefebvre, *Rhythmanalysis*, 78.

a bounded place over which we struggle and toward *urbaniza-tion* as flexible social fabrics that connect complex ecologies of labor and capital, transportation and communication networks, different groups and societies, and so on.[24] The urban is formless, not a physical entity but the process and product of encounters: "the sheer proximity of people to other people," Andy Merrifield announces, "the sheer simultaneity of activities, of events and chance meetings, *is the very definition of urban society itself.*"[25] The city as a built environment remains even as it changes (decays or grows or stagnates), but the urban is the *assembling* of different networks across space and time. As urbanization produces form-less spaces partially and ephemerally through encounters, capi-talism moves from being organized around and for linear dom-ination and toward "relative" and even lived differences, which implies that "space and time are themselves capitalist constructs, and the mass and velocity of commodities, of capital and money shifting around the market universe, creates its own bending and warping of time and space, its own space-time dimensionality."[26] The scale and reach of urbanization today are truly planetary and outshine our sensory and intellectual capacities.

These changes, condensed in the conceptual move from Fordism to post-Fordism, ironically accomplished Lefebvre's project. Without recognizing capital's incorporation of Lefe-bvre's demand, we can't properly map the contemporary peda-gogical and political rhythms of exploitation, oppression, and resistance. Post-Fordism expropriates the interminable reforma-

---

24   Henri Lefebvre, *The Urban Revolution*, trans. R. Bononno (Minneapolis: University of Minnesota Press, 1970/2003).

25   Merrifield, *The Politics of the Encounter*, 37.

26   Ibid., 7.

tion of space and time, finding sources of accumulation in perpetual appropriations as it absorbs détournement within capital's logic. Under post-Fordism, détournement—the opening of unforeseen and uncalculated desires, events, and knowledges—is subsumed under the demand for production and actualization such that it's no longer a sharp break or a real sensation of the possibility of revolutionary struggle.[27] As Rockhill writes, "if the development of artistic practice has shown anything, it is not simply that there are always new rules to be broken. It is that rule breaking has become a norm."[28] Under post-Fordism, capital profits from both cyclical and linear repetitions so long as they *create* something new. Lefebvre's project to overturn the domination of linear over cyclical rhythms is completed under post-Fordism, but without the emancipatory possibilities for which he hoped.

The problem is not so much the relationship between linear and cyclical repetitions, but capital's aptitude for appropriating both—under the demand of production—in its dynamic perceptual ecology. Under post-Fordism, the moment of détournement is sutured tightly between domination and appropriation. Returning to the rhythms of debt, think about how debt fundamentally alters our sense and understanding of time, which is most evident in its tyranny over our free time. We're compelled to "quantify and measure even our moments of leisure time," as we necessarily trade leisure—and the interest we accumulate as a result—for productivity.[29] Alternatively,

---

27   Ford, *Marxism, Pedagogy, and the General Intellect.*

28   Rockhill, *Radical History and the Politics of Art,* 123.

29   Jason Wozniak, "Creating the Conditions for Free Time in the Debt Economy: On Stealing Time in and Through Education," *Philosoph-*

we might think about how the incessant demand to produce doesn't so much limit leisure time as frame it, such that time spent not working ultimately serves the function of making us more productive workers. Capital today *wants* us to détourn, to do the unexpected, to self-actualize and manage our entrepreneurial selves, to maximize our productivity and efficiency for flexible and continuous improvement. There's nothing capital wants more than innovation; the blank dots on the page exist to be filled in new and creative ways.

This is not to say that capital's accommodation of creativity is *novel* per se. As far back as the *Manifesto of the Communist Party*, Marx and Engels observed that the creation of the new is the motor of capitalism: "the bourgeoisie cannot exist without constantly revolutionizing the instruments of production, and thereby the relations of production, and with them the whole relations of society."[30] To be sure, "the constant differentiation of space is necessary to the very survival of capitalism" because differences result in new values.[31] What *is* unique to post-Fordism is the enormous flexibility of capital to profit from differential spaces and, as I've shown, diverse and new rhythms. The real question, then, might be: Can we rethink Lefebvre's rhythmanalysis in such a way that détournement is redeemed and cyclical repetitions aren't oriented toward development?

---

ical Inquiry in Education 29, no. 2 (2022): 118.

30   Karl Marx and Friedrich Engels, *The Communist Manifesto*, trans. S. Moore (New York: Penguin, 1848/1967), 222.

31   Don Mitchell, *Mean Streets: Homelessness, Public Space, and the Limits of Capital* (Athens: The University of Georgia Press, 2020), 98.

In the concluding section of *Rhythmanalysis*, Lefebvre delineates the components of rhythmanalysis. The body is always polyrhythmic in that it "is composed of diverse rhythms" and it is "eurythmic" in that it "presupposes" polyrhythms yet unites them to produce a "normal" body.[32] Polyrhythms allow for the combination of linear and cyclical repetitions.

The last component is *arrhythmia*: the gap introduced into any rhythm, measure, or combination thereof. "In arrhythmia," he bemoans, "rhythms break apart, alter and bypass *synchronization*."[33] Arrhythmia is a sickness in need of *preventative* cures that can synthesize a polyrhythmic society where multiple rhythms coexist. Post-Fordism is the capitalist manifestation of a polyrhythmic society. Differential rhythms and knowledge produce new value for accumulation exactly by preventatively treating arrhythmia. From this, it follows that an arrhythmic pedagogy might immobilize or at least challenge contemporary capitalist accumulation and imperialist domination. Capitalism is a rhythmic process of and between investment, production, and realization, and crises are constituted by the breach of these rhythms, their breaking apart: arrhythmia.

Wozniak innovatively reads Lefebvre against Lefebvre, arguing that arrhythmic disruptions can "create lacunae or holes in hegemonic temporalities [...] by suspending processes of exchange-value production."[34] Building on Wozniak's thesis, I take arrhythmia as a pause of unlearning that can become political if the perceptual ecology of capital that détournement suspends

---

32   Lefebvre, *Rhythmanalysis*, 77.

33   Ibid., 77.

34   Wozniak, "Towards a Rhythmanalysis of Debt Dressage," 504.

can be sustained through an aesthetic experience in the actuality of revolution. Teaching the actuality of revolution can enact détournement as a *break* between domination and appropriation, an interruption that we struggle to sustain and foster. If linear repetition is rational and planned, and if cyclical repetition entails a new opening that's always in the process of becoming, then perhaps the arrhythmic is the opening to an enduring détournement that can't be captured because it suspends production, remaining a potentiality without any actualization.

It is not so much that Lefebvre's rhythmanalysis is incorrect or unjust in its desire for differential space-time but that it's predicated on the developmental logic of post-Fordism that insists on endless becoming. While the infinity of becoming seems weightless, untethered to tradition, norms, or economic obstacles, it still rests on "an underlying determinism and developmentalism that is no different from the neoliberal, entrepreneurial self that is equally interested in continual self-fashioning, self-stylization, and self-overcoming."[35] For the economy of learning, arrhythmia is indeed an illness halting, delaying, or otherwise disrupting the self's constant redevelopment.

Lefebvre's rhythmanalysis lends itself to a constant generation of knowledge and understanding to change the world, to reclaim the use-value of the cyclical repetitions of lived bodies from the exchange-value of the linear rhythms of capital and the state. Under contemporary capital, rhythmanalysis ultimately produces new data, information, and knowledge for capital to expropriate and valorize. The system develops our skills to hear and listen for new and different things, a development that occurs according to the regime of recognition. We could recuper-

---

35   Lewis, *Inoperative Learning*, 38.

ate arrhythmanalysis as a rupture opening the space and time for unlearning.

The pedagogical rhythms of unlearning are not only open to but *defined* by interruptions, kinks, and new beginnings. The temporal breaches can undo any prior accumulation. As the pedagogy of cyclical repetition, unlearning disables the ever-shifting beginning and endpoints that define the linear repetitions of learning. By reasserting the centrality of arrhythmia to cyclical repetition, interruptions are set loose from new developments so that the caesura of détournement can persist long enough for us to sense a radically different aesthetic regime and revolutionary possibility. Under post-Fordism, the pedagogical task of resistance is to suspend the mind's normal functioning. This might happen through *arrhythmic* disruptions, pedagogical moments of suspension that *hold open* the gap of détournement. The subversive potential of such moments appears in stark relief when we consider just how important it is for capital's urbanist pedagogy of learning to either close or orient our perceptual capacities away from such scissions. One case in point is the ongoing history of "ugly laws" or "unsightly beggar laws" in U.S. cities (and those under U.S. control), a complex set of ordinances that criminalize the very presence of certain bodies behaving in particular ways in public. Especially illustrative here are injunctions against public epileptic seizures because, as Susan Schweik writes, "epilepsy stops the city's business forever, or at any rate constitutes it as a perpetual horror."[36]

To what extent is it possible for the teacher to *point* at an element of any rhythmic repetition? Unlike sight, sound is ephem-

---

36   Susan M. Schweik, *The Ugly Laws: Disability in Public* (New York: New York University Press, 2009), 89.

eral and fleeting, reverberating and resonating, and difficult to pin down. We can point to a recording and say: listen to *this*, but the *this* to which we refer isn't located exactly by the point, the pointer, or the pointed-to. Insofar as sounds are vibrations, movements in migration, or echoes that are always moving on and beyond, listening is elusive. The inability to locate sound is an adequate example of how the teacher's intentions enacted through the gesture of pointing are oriented toward the facilitation of encounters that exceed any lesson plan or scripted curriculum. The teacher points students to something, but no amount of precise verbiage or scaffolding properly designates the "this" to which the teacher points, as sound is, by definition, always in movement. Pointing inaugurates an arrhythmic puncture in the ceaseless repetitions of the now. Détournement provides a pedagogical and political opening by providing the conditions for appropriation as a fact to be accomplished, which can nurture our ability to sense and know the possibilities of the past and future.

REVISING LEFEBVRE'S PROJECT

Lefebvre's thought leaves an important legacy for understanding and intervening in the capitalist abstraction of work, space, and time, one we should build and modify. The argument articulated in this chapter is mostly pedagogical and could certainly appear as a romanticization of arrhythmia, which is not valuable or politically useful in itself. Instead, the pedagogy of arrhythmic unlearning is political in the context of teaching the actuality of revolution in our conjuncture. To close this chapter, I correct three errors necessary for bringing Lefebvre's rhythmanalysis to bear on any revolutionary aesthetic education today.

The first revision has to do with Lefebvre's theory of revolution: an endless process of temporary détournements and "a permanent cultural revolution."[37] Lefebvre supplements the revolution with subversion. "Revolution," he asserts, "acts on the political level, and subversion acts to destroy the political."[38] His vision is one where orders are created and undermined continually until we reach communism. Revolution isn't an acute shift but takes place "by imprinting a **rhythm** on an era" neither by armed force nor by political or theoretical struggle, but over a long duration so that, "a long time after the action, one sees the emergence of novelty."[39] This is the basis on which Lefebvre dismisses and denunciates the actually-existing socialist projects of his time. Beginning in the 1960s, Łukasz Stanek notes, "Lefebvre described the post-Stalinist socialist states in the same way as he described capitalist states."[40] It was most explicit in his later theory of the State Mode of Production, which collapses radically different social forms—from fascism and social democracy to capitalism and socialism—together.

Lefebvre opposed these states insofar as each "plans and organizes society 'rationally,'" thus "imposing analogous, if not homologous, measures irrespective of political ideology, historical

---

37   Henri Lefebvre, *Writings on Cities*, trans. E. Kofman and E. Lebas (Malden: Blackwell, 1996), 180.

38   Lefebvre, *Towards an Architecture of Enjoyment*, 73.

39   Lefebvre, *Rhythmanalysis*, 24, bold in original.

40   Łukasz Stanek, *Henri Lefebvre on Space: Architecture, Urban Research, and the Production of Theory* (Minneapolis: University of Minnesota Press, 2011), 64.

background, or the class origins of those in power."[41] Lefebvre's critiques of capitalism were as consistent and frequent as those of socialist projects. Malott, for instance, cites a lecture from the 1960s that "begins by arguing that all political programs [...] either work within or against the state."[42] The latter strategy is the only correct one for Lefebvre, and it's organized around events, moments, or *everyday* resistances that provide experiments in *autogestion*, a term designating the small-scale democratic control of producing and reproducing life. In the place of either "political change at the level of the state or [...] the collective or state ownership of the means of production," revolution entails "a collective ownership and management of space founded on the permanent participation of the 'interested parties,' with their multiple, varied and even contradictory interests."[43] The political problem in Lefebvre's project is the sweeping *theoretical abstraction* from the political conjuncture. Revolutions don't entail taking state power, large-scale organizations like parties, or even social planning. This is not to say that revolutions are *only* defined by these three tasks, of course, but that they are definitional of revolution. The second revision, then, is to pursue a contingent and dialectic strategy of détournement, appropriation, and organization instead of separating them as Lefebvre does.

Finally, although Lefebvre correctly insists that "a revolution that does not produce a new space has not realized its full potential; indeed, it has failed in that it has not changed life it-

---

41 Lefebvre, *The Production of Space*, 23.

42 Curry Malott, "Vindicating Stalin: Responding to Lefebvre," *Policy Futures in Education* 15, no. 4 (2017): 443.

43 Lefebvre, *The Production of Space*, 422.

self," he incorrectly states that socialism didn't produce any new spaces.[44] The third modification is to reclaim the legacy of the workers' struggle, with all its tragedies and accomplishments. The socialist project *has*, through organized and even large-scale détournements, produced spaces of appropriation where use-value has the upper hand over exchange-value and where difference reigned over abstraction. The mass-built housing projects in Lefebvre's homeland of France and the Soviet Union may have appeared similar, but "mass housing across the Soviet Union [...] was, despite the appearance of monotony, in fact substantively diverse."[45] These differences manifested rhythmically throughout the socialist experiment. Even large-scale planned units were "subject to constant change over time and modification into intricate arrays of sub-types."[46]

Networks of different cities had distinct forms of producing and reproducing the social. Beginning in the 1950s, what the Soviets called microdistricts "described neighborhood-scale urban territory that existed in this network and encapsulated the multiscalar correspondence of parts of the single entity."[47] Each housed between 5,000-10,000 people and included schools, hospitals, libraries, parks, and more. Different social groups, from factory workers to Party elites, lived in the same housing units and microdistricts. Contrary to "the increasingly troubled council estates of Britain or the housing projects of the United

44 Lefebvre, *The Production of Space*, 54.

45 Murawski, "Actually-Existing Success," 928.

46 Ibid.

47 Kimberly Elman Zarecor, "What was so Socialist about the Socialist City? Second World Urbanity in Europe," *Journal of Urban History* 44, no. 1 (2018): 102.

States, all kinds of people lived in Soviet microdistricts, bringing traditional family and neighborhood rhythms to complement and clash with those of proto-communist organization."[48] This is not to romanticize Soviet microdistricts, but to identify how planning and organization, when done collectively, can create— and *have* created—a radically different perceptual ecology deeply related to the organization of space and time around use value and encounters with differences.

Defending détournement and holding open the moment of stupidity challenges the domination of exchange-value. Arrhythmic pedagogy of and for the unthought is oriented *not* to render it knowable but to preserve its ineffability. It encompasses sketching out and listening for the paused moment of détournement required for a revolutionary break and appropriation, one that breaks through the temporal prison that urgentism produces by "simultaneously obliterating the past and transforming the future into an endless repetition of what exists *here* and *now*."[49] While I've tried to get at the excess of cyclical and linear repetitions and the surplus of thought in this chapter, this shouldn't be interpreted as an uncritical celebration of either or as an argument *against* repetition or knowledge. Ephemerality, uncertainty, and planning should be neither uncritically celebrated nor elevated against each other. At the same time, under the rhythmic capture of post-Fordism, without attending to the arrhythmic, we're more susceptible to returning to the circuits of capital. Arrhythmanalysis, then, is a *strategic* pedagogy that can supplement the theoretical resources Lefebvre provides us in

48   Ibid., 109.

49   Rockhill, "Temporal Economies and the Prison of the Present," 17.

our ongoing fight against capitalist abstraction, helping us listen for what we don't know.

CONCLUSION

(UN)LEARNING THROUGH PERCEPTUAL MEANING

Ideology functions as a map of the social world, a representation of the conscious and unconscious imaginary relations we have to our real-life processes. In the first chapter, I argued that implicit in Rockhill's project to rethink and reenact the politics of art is a pedagogical problematic of mapping, or "charting out the immanent force fields of activity" operating to determine what politics, art, and political art are in any conjuncture.[1] To conclude, I return to the need for a political, aesthetic, and educational cartography of the immanent forces at work in our conjuncture by advancing a final pedagogical practice: perceptual mapping.

In the early 1980s, Jameson posited cognitive mapping as an explicitly aesthetic and pedagogical project to address the abandonment of the work of art as a work of teaching. "The pedagogical function of a work of art," he begins one speech, "seems

---

1   Rockhill, *Radical History and the Politics of Art*, 235.

in various forms to have been an inescapable parameter of any conceivable Marxist aesthetic."[2] The teaching function of art is an inevitable defining feature of marxist theory and the marxist movement because both require a certain sensation of the totality of capitalism and the creation of a new perception of socialism and the socialist struggle. Jameson's intervention responded to an ideological crisis in marxism stemming from the lack of "a vision of the future that grips the masses," a crisis with only a few exceptions (Jameson cites Cuba and the Socialist Federal Republic of Yugoslavia).[3] Cognitive mapping addresses the need for revolutionary marxism to connect the revolutionary subject and the revolutionary project, a theme clear in Jameson's earlier work.[4]

Jameson gets cognitive mapping from Kevin Lynch's 1960 book, *The Image of the City*. In that book, Lynch examines "the visual quality of the American city by studying the mental image of that city which is held by its citizens," focusing especially on its transparency, or the "ease with which its parts can be recognized and can be organized into a coherent pattern."[5] Finding that most people couldn't imagine the city as a totality, Lynch's work proposes how to overcome this deficiency. Jameson adds the political context Lynch neglected, bringing in Ernest Man-

2   Fredric Jameson, "Cognitive Mapping," in L. Grossberg and C. Nelson (Eds.), *Marxism and the Interpretation of Culture* (Chicago: University of Illinois Press, 1988), 347.

3   Ibid., 355.

4   See Fredric Jameson, *Marxism and Form: Twentieth-Century Dialectical Theories of Literature* (Princeton: Princeton University Press, 1971), xvii-xviii.

5   Kevin Lynch, *The Image of the City* (Cambridge: The MIT Press, 1960), 2-3.

del's theory of "late capitalism," in which our daily lives, knowledge, and perceptions are increasingly disconnected from or opaque within the overall totality of the capitalist system. The development of capital's totality, the various forms it takes, and the flexible accumulation strategies we've charted throughout this book, make our global condition beyond our individual reach. As a result, the capitalist totality we live in and produce is "ultimately unrepresentable or [...] something like an absent cause, one that can never emerge into the presence of perception" but that "can find figures through which to express itself in distorted and symbolic ways."[6] Cognitive mapping embraces our inability to locate ourselves within the totality and proposes to think the unthinkable: to map the totality.

Totality is different from totalization. Totality refers to the entirety of the world *as it exists,* and totalization refers to the attempt to *sense* and *know* that totality. That totality is unknowable doesn't mean we shouldn't *strive* for it, because at the very least we can better locate our local realities within the global processes that produce them. Consider the shift from the city to the urban in the last chapter. The city was a comprehensible and definable entity, while the urban is formless and global, something that, in Merrifield's words, "outstrips our cognitive and sensory facilities; the mind boggles at the sensory overload that today's urban process places upon us."[7] We have to link wondering—or the mind boggling—with possibility as the class struggle demands we better identify the totality of capitalism, locate ourselves and our struggles within it, and figure the unrepresentable totality of a future communist society that can provide further

---

6   Jameson, "Cognitive Mapping," 350.

7   Merrifield, *The Politics of the Encounter,* 5.

inspiration for and ammunition in the revolutionary project.

FROM COGNITIVE TO PERCEPTUAL MAPPING

Although he doesn't reference Jameson's work or cognitive mapping, I want to link both with McLaren, especially his early work, published well before his turn to marxism. In *Schooling as Ritual Performance*, McLaren analyzes the formal educational institution and "*classroom instruction itself* as a ritualized transaction."[8] McLaren calls at the end of the book for the development of "a theory of cultural analysis—which I refer to as cultural cartography." Mapping must "engage students—by way of 'semiotic guerilla warfare'" and sketch "contemporary social life in all its cleavage and continuity, rupture and bland consensus" by "paying precise and consistent attention to the ways in which larger representations of power [...] are inseparably bonded to rituals."[9] Gestures, for example, not only *represent* but *enflesh* feelings and social relations so that "gestures of resistance *are* student anger, fear, and refusal expressed in an incarnate or corporeal mode," including the frequent "resistant" gestures like "leaning back on chairs [...] lullingly sitting at your desk and looking around the room with a bored expression [...] wearing 'intimidating' clothing."[10]

Such gestures and their materialization of ideological conditions can't be understood without locating them within the overall social and political economy of meaning and, as he'll later add, capitalist value production. What's noteworthy is that McLaren early on also linked theory with aesthetic processes,

---

8   McLaren, *Schooling as Ritual Performance*, 25.

9   Ibid., 260, 261.

10   Ibid., 149, 150.

even if it would take him some time to connect these to political economy. Only later could he assist Grande in her fight against those who would cast aside "the real sites of struggle (sovereignty and self-determination)" in American Indian communities with "identity politics" and "the current obsession with questions of identity and authenticity."[11] It was in this phase that McLaren's cultural cartography could pursue the marxist political project.

The pedagogical and aesthetic dimensions of cognitive mapping join contemporary investigation with utopian imagination. "An aesthetic of cognitive mapping" is, Jameson says at one point, "a pedagogical political culture which seeks to endow the individual subject with some new heightened sense of its place in the global system" and "will necessarily have to respect this now enormously complex representation dialectic."[12] Cognitive mapping is intellectual—in that it requires the competency to name and locate aspects of the totality—and aesthetic—in that it motivates imaginaries beyond capitalism via the sense of the map, which presents not determinate but partial knowledge as well as future and present possibilities for liberation.

Jameson is clear that the pedagogical function of the aesthetic must be redeemed, although he never specifies the pedagogical dimension of the aesthetics of cognitive mapping. He does, however, offer two hints. The first clue is in his introductory statements to his speech on cognitive mapping from 1983: "I am addressing a subject about which I know nothing whatsoever, except for the fact that it does not exist."[13] His admitted

---

11   Grande, *Red Pedagogy*, 138.

12   Fredric Jameson, "Postmodernism, or the Cultural Logic of Late Capitalism," *New Left Review* 1, no. 146 (1984): 92.

13   Jameson, "Cognitive Mapping," 347.

ignorance is a performance of his process of unlearning as well as an admission of the impossibility of generating knowledge and the necessity of remaining within *thought*. The second clue is in his book on Bertolt Brecht, where he defines teaching, as we did in the second chapter, as "less a mimesis of scientific knowledge [...] than it is the representation of how you go about transmitting and conveying such knowledge." "Teaching is thus showing," and "the dramatic representation of teaching is the showing of showing, the showing of how you show and demonstrate."[14] Teaching is not just pointing, then, but pointing to pointing. Cognitive mapping has the pedagogical function of showing and critiquing what exists—pointing to a particular representation of the totality—and what escapes sensation—pointing to pointing. What are the pedagogical functions of showing and sensing what exists, what escapes sensation, the critique of the present, the imagination of the future, and the sensation that the world can be radically otherwise?

To account for the historical production of the organization of our sensual regimes and worlds, I want to unlearn the well-documented dominance of the visual in much of our world. Jameson's cognitive mapping, like Lynch's mapping of the cityscape from which it's inspired, only concerns sight and only engages sight through the eye, insufficiently accounting for the historical production of our sensorial regimes and content. The mapping I sketch and enact doesn't isolate or privilege any particular sense, but allows for various interactions, orders, and reorganizations of our senses. In this way, I listen to how Fred Moten lets the voice of organized Black communists interrupt

---

14   Fredric Jameson, *Brecht and Method* (New York: Verso, 2000), 91.

Jameson's mapping project, which not only engages mapping as a multisensorial endeavor but, at the same time, also returns the visual from the grips of the eye's gaze.

In a foundational article on cognitive mapping, Jameson mentions the League of Revolutionary Black Workers, a Black communist organization founded in Detroit in 1969 that, within only a few years, made tremendous gains in industrial workplaces through wildcat strikes. The League's ultimate defeat and dissolution justify the need for cognitive mapping. He acknowledges the League's remarkable successes, how it managed to take over workplaces, create new counter-media apparatuses to challenge and divide the corporate-owned presses, and even intervene effectively in local elections. While Jameson is clear that the League was "the single most significant political experience of the American 1960s," their project failed because they couldn't appreciate or represent Detroit within the totality of global capital.[15] As they began traveling across the globe to build and study with different organizations, networks, and communities, they moved onto a more global scale of time and space as their local project petered out. This signals "the problem of representation," particularly "how to represent a unique local model and experience to people in other situations."[16] The totality of capital overcame their struggle.

Jameson's reference for the League is the book *Detroit: I Do Mind Dying* by historians Dan Georgakis and Marvin Surkin instead of *Finally Got the News*, the film directed by Stewart Bird, Rene Lichtman, and Peter Gessner in collaboration with the League. Thus, Jameson's critique isn't of the League itself but

15   Jameson, "Cognitive Mapping," 351.

16   Ibid., 352.

of the way Georgakis and Surkin represent it. Fred Moten takes Jameson's opening as an opportunity to engage the League's self-representation. Listening to the film, Moten points to a critical audible moment in the film when the "lectural voice" of League leader Kenneth Cockrel sounds out over images of factory workers. Because Cockrel's voice is acousmatic—meaning that it "emerges from an off-screen source" that can't be identified—but is juxtaposed over images of factory workers, it "holds forth precisely on totality, on the nature of the world order and the League's position within it."[17]

It is important to note Moten's decision to term Cockrel's acousmatic appearance as a "lectural voice" precisely because of our association of the lecture with the presentation of certain knowledge. Cockrel's sonic appearance aligns with the pedagogical logic of cognitive mapping as it forces us to question the certainty typically associated with the visual but without abandoning all pretense to knowledge. As Moten writes, "the operations of certain sonic elements in *Finally Got the News* move within the project of representing and transforming postmodern global space while keeping in mind the fact that such operations [...] are partial and preliminary." Acousmatic sound works to connect discordant spaces of the totality while itself remaining disconnected from any particular location, which is why the sonic elements of the film "transform representation into a synaesthetic substitute for vision—wherein a narrative of defeat turns into a projection of victory."[18] The League didn't fail to represent the revolutionary struggle in its totality, didn't lack the ability to lo-

17   Fred Moten, *In the Break: The Aesthetics of the Black Radical Tradition* (Minneapolis: University of Minnesota Press, 2003), 220.

18   Ibid., 221.

cate their struggle within the uncertain and shifting coordinates of capitalism; Jameson failed to *listen* for it. Locating ourselves, even visually, isn't only a matter of the eye. Thinking of cognitive mapping as an educational project to produce representations of the totality by engaging multisensorial modalities and recognizing the partiality and limitations of knowledge justifies a shift toward the language of perceptual mapping.

(Un)Learning Through Perceptual Mapping

More than a tool, perceptual mapping serves as a model for teaching the actuality of revolution through (un)learning, an example of a pedagogical process through which we unlearn capital's perceptual ecology and not only learn the possibility of alternative sensoriums, but actively construct and experience them. As we work to develop, chart out, and diagram an impossible totality, we learn and encounter the perceptual schema of capital and how it produces fits and misfits between ourselves and the world. Through that effort, we unlearn the perceptual order associated with the maps we have in our heads already. By experiencing our inability to grasp the world, to listen only for what we know or can know, we surrender the pretense of discovery and self-accumulation, or the possibility of conclusively knowing the entirety of the international working class we're interacting with every time we exchange commodities or money.

The pedagogy of perceptual mapping is distinct from its politics in that the educational impact of unlearning is a détournement without a new appropriation, while the political project is always a new revolutionary appropriation.[19] In our con-

---

19   See Tyson E. Lewis, "Too Little, Too Late: Reflections on Fredric Jameson's Pedagogy of Form," *Rethinking Marxism* 21, no. 3 (2009):

juncture, pedagogy is an experience of the gaps in the world, of the past and future within the present, of the void between the ahistorical time of capital and the Historical time of revolution. Marxist politics is the project of assembling the forces to bridge that void. Both are conditioned by the actuality of revolution insofar as the pedagogical objective of generating experiences of another perceptual regime—through which we disidentify with capital–and the political objective of creating a new perceptual regime are both determined by the revolutionary fact to be accomplished.

(Un)learning in perceptual mapping poses problems *and* solutions, produces knowledge *and* thought, works on affective and cognitive levels to let us sense capital's ecology more accurately, and provides an entry point into a different perceptual regime of sense-making. It works to not only identify the shifting boundaries of and locations within the totality but, more importantly, to germinate possible revolutionary visions of a radically transformed society. Such mapping should serve the *political* struggle by addressing "the enormous strategic and tactical difficulties of coordinating local and grassroots or neighborhood political actions with national or international ones" as they "are all immediately functions of the enormously complex new international space."[20] To act—individually and collectively—we must be able to sense and have some knowledge about the various coordinates in which we operate and by which we're determined. By teaching—or by *pointing* to—the gap between the knowledge and the object of perceptual maps, the arrhythmic disruptions of alternative perceptual ecologies sound out.

438-452.

   20   Jameson, "Cognitive Mapping," 351.

We form new political ideas and beliefs and construct new his-
torically-determined ways of sensing.

Here, we see that the distinction I drew in the first chapter
between education as description and as demonstration might
not be so hard and fast as the aesthetics of education become
political. Through perceptual mapping, we create more comprehensive and accessible *critiques* and *descriptions* of the fundamental and common problems at the heart of the oppression
and suffering of our diverse and international class, *accounts*
of the contradictions on which we can seize, and *proposals* for
the most appropriate tactics and strategies to deploy within
the most correct ideological framework. Perceptual maps *think*
through the problem of revolution "politically—that is to say, as
a contradiction in reality that cannot be removed by thought,
but only by reality."[21] They organize *experiences* to unlearn our
assigned roles in capital's totality and encourage the sensation
that another totality is possible through enduring the divisions
and limitations of our perceptions and descriptions. They help
us *think* about the aesthetics of our explanations, conceiving and
experiencing them as cartographic clefts of disidentification,
teaching us a different sensorial regime as we learn to listen to
the silences in the current one and let alternative sensorial orders
emit their neglected and repressed sensorial matter.

Our goal is, like Marx's, to effect a perceptual shift in ourselves and others such that we emerge from the text or protest,
classroom or rally, as subjects with different relations to the capitalist totality and the communist struggle. Situated within the
educational project of teaching the actuality of revolution, perceptual mapping and (un)learning more broadly identifies the

---

21   Althusser, *Machiavelli and Us*, 80.

breaks within our world, teaching us the possibility of producing other, revolutionary breaks.

ACKNOWLEDGEMENTS

Although I've been trying to take some time off from writing this past year, a certain combination of contingencies compelled me to engage in the research and thinking presented in—and conducted through—this book, unexpected encounters with friends and comrades, students and colleagues, ideas and concepts, political issues and movements. One decisive moment, which came from my political activities, was reading the work of comrades Jennifer Ponce de León and Gabriel Rockhill. Their work on aesthetics and politics energized me and made me reevaluate my own educational and political theories and practices. At the same time, I was studying the aesthetics of teaching with my student Daniela Chaparro just after researching the sonic dimensions of the class struggle with another student, Maria Esposito. Some of my research with Chaparro appears in the first two chapters.

I was fortunately subjected to a few encounters in academia that really took hold. One was with Peter McLaren, who generously offered to serve on my dissertation committee in 2015 and hasn't stopped stimulating me to think more precisely about the relationship between marxism, pedagogy, and social movements since. A second was with Tyson Lewis, who let me gain a footing in the aesthetics of education. A third was with Curry Malott, Brad Porfilio, and Bill Reynolds, who each interpellated me as a serious thinker and helped clear space in our field for revolutionary praxis. A fourth encounter that fundamentally changed my life was the incidental way I met Sarah Pfohl in 2012. For 10 years now, she's taught me so much about teaching, art, and how to generally be a better presence in the world. Finally, the most immediate chance event that sparked this book came in a panel discussion about *Encountering Education*, when Jason Wozniak pointed out that I hadn't considered the *teacher* in relation to pedagogy.

In terms of the words that appear on these pages, and the convictions, critiques, and aspirations they convey, I owe a great deal of thanks to those who read over early versions of individual chapters and the manuscript in its entirety, including Summer Pappachen, Tyson Lewis, David Backer (who pointed me to the silent score of ideology), Jennifer Ponce de León, Petar Jandrić, E. Wayne Ross, and some anonymous reviewers with *Postdigital Science and Education*, *Critical Education*, and the *International Journal of Education Through Art*.

Others accidentally provided ideas, problems, and other resources evident in this book: Sandy Grande, Nazia Kazi, Kym Smyth, Hannah Dickinson, Nino Brown, Noah Roberts, Radhika Desai, Layan Fuleihan, Wayne Au, Glenn Rikowski, Dave Hill, Joris Vlieghe, Piotr Zamoiski, and students in my Spring 2022 "Education, Space, and Urban Revolutions" class (who, along with me, suffered through my book on space and pedagogy). So too did those in and around the Hampton Institute, International Manifesto Group, Geopolitical Economy Research Group, the Center for Communist Studies, the Critical Theory Workshop, the People's Forum, and the Indianapolis Liberation Center.

The team at Iskra was incredibly supportive throughout the writing and revision process, reading multiple drafts multiple times for content and form. It's such a joy to publish with comrades who are interested in the content and have a stake in the struggles in which it intervenes, and take so much effort and care in feedback, copyediting, design, promotion, and more.

BIBLIOGRAPHY

Allman, Paula. *Critical Education Against Global Capitalism: Karl Marx and Revolutionary Education*. Rotterdam: Sense, 2010.

Althusser, Louis. *For Marx*. Trans. B. Brewster. New York: Verso, 1965/2005.

Althusser, Louis. "From *Capital* to Marx's Philosophy." In L. Althusser, É. Balibar, R. Establet, P. Macherey, and J. Rancière, *Reading Capital*. Trans. B. Brewster and D. Fernbach. New York: Verso, 1965/2015.

Althusser, Louis. *History and Imperialism: Writings, 1963-1986*. Trans. G.M. Goshgarian. Cambridge: Polity Press, 2018/2020.

Althusser, Louis. *How to be a Marxist in Philosophy*. Trans. G.M. Goshgarian. London: Bloomsbury, 2015/2017.

Althusser, Louis. *Lenin and Philosophy and Other Essays*. Trans. B. Brewster. New York: Monthly Review Press, 1971/2001.

Althusser, Louis. *Machiavelli and Us*. Trans. F. Matheron. New York: Verso, 2000.

Althusser, Louis. *On the Reproduction of Capitalism*. Ed. J. Bidet.

Trans. B. Brewster and G.M. Goshgarian. New York: Verso, 1995/2014.

Althusser, Louis. *Philosophy for Non-Philosophers*. Trans. G.M. Goshgarian. London: Bloomsbury, 2014/2017.

Althusser, Louis. *Philosophy of the Encounter: Later Writings, 1978-1987*. Trans. G.M. Goshgarian. New York: Verso, 1993/2006.

Althusser, Louis. "Reply to John Lewis." In L. Althusser, *On Ideology*. New York: Verso, 1971/2008.

Althusser, Louis. "The Object of *Capital*." In L. Althusser, É. Balibar, R. Establet, P. Macherey, and J. Rancière, *Reading Capital*. Trans. B. Brewster and D. Fernbach. New York: Verso, 1965/2015.

Althusser, Louis. *What is to be Done?* Trans. G.M. Goshgarian. Cambridge: Polity Press, 2018/2020.

Au, Wayne, *A Marxist Education: Learning to Change the World*. Chicago: Haymarket Books, 2018.

Azoulay, Ariella Aïsha. *Potential History: Unlearning Imperialism*. New York: Verso, 2019.

Backer, David I. "History of the Reproduction-Resistance Dichotomy in Critical Education: The Line of Critique against Louis Althusser, 1974-1985." *Critical Education* 12, no. 6 (2021): 1-21.

Backer, David I. *The Gold and the Dross: Althusser for Educators*. Boston: Brill, 2019.

Becker, Brian. "Introduction: The Importance of the 100th Anniversary of the Russian Revolution." In *Storming the Gates: How the Russian Revolution Changed the World*. Ed. J. Cutter. San Francisco: Liberation Media, 2017.

Becker, Brian. "Praxis: Revolutionary Theory and Practice in the Present." In *Keywords in Radical Philosophy and Education: Common Concepts for Contemporary Movements*. Ed. D.R. Ford. Boston: Brill, 2019.

Biesta, Gert J.J. *The Beautiful Risk of Education*. Boulder: Paradigm Publishers, 2014.

Biesta, Gert J.J. *The Rediscovery of Teaching*. New York: Routledge, 2017.

Biesta, Gert J.J. *World-Centered Education: A View for the Present*. New York: Routledge, 2022.

Bowles, Samuel and Herbert Gintis. *Schooling in Capitalist America: Educational Reform and the Contradictions of Economic Life*. New York: Basic Books, 1976.

Boxley, Simon. "ESC in the Anthropocene: Education for Sustainability and Communism." *Critical Education* 13, no. 1 (2022): 51-69.

Davis, Colin. "Althusser on Reading and Self-Reading." *Textual Practice* 15, no. 2 (2001): 299-316.

Dean, Jodi. "The Actuality of Revolution." In *Storming the Gates: How the Russian Revolution Changed the World*. Ed. J. Cutter. San Francisco: Liberation Media, 2017.

Dickinson, Hannah, and Curry Malott. "What is Alienation? The Development and Legacy of Marx's Early Theory." *Liberation School*, 07 December 2021. Available here: https://www.liberationschool.org/13-what-is-alienation-html.

Dolmage, Jay Timothy. *Academic Ableism: Disability and Higher Education*. Ann Arbor: University of Michigan Press, 2017.

Ford, Derek R. *Communist Study: Education for the Commons*, 2nd ed. Lanham: Lexington Books, 2022.

Ford, Derek R. *Encountering Education: Elements for a Marxist Pedagogy*. Madison: Iskra Books, 2022.

Ford, Derek R. *Inhuman Educations: Jean-François Lyotard, Pedagogy, Thought*. Boston: Brill, 2021.

Ford, Derek R. *Marxism, Pedagogy, and the General Intellect: Beyond the Knowledge Economy*. New York: Palgrave Macmillan, 2021.

Ford, Derek R. *Politics and Pedagogy in the "Post-Truth" Era: Insurgent Philosophy and Praxis*. London: Bloomsbury, 2019.

Freire, Paulo. *Education for Critical Consciousness*. London: Continuum, 1974/2015.

Freire, Paulo. *Pedagogy of the Oppressed*. Trans. M.B. Ramos. New York: Continuum, 1970/2011.

Genovese, Taylor R. "Translator's Introduction." In A. Bogdanov, *Art and the Working Class*. Trans. T.R. Genovese. Madison: Iskra Books, 2022.

Grande, Sandy. *Red Pedagogy: Native American Social and Political Thought*, 10th anniversary ed. Lanham: Rowman & Littlefield, 2004/2015.

Harvey, David. "History Versus Theory: A Commentary on Marx's Method in *Capital*." *Historical Materialism* 20, no. 2 (2012): 3-38.

Harvey, David. "The 'New' Imperialism: Accumulation by Dispossession." *Socialist Register* 40 (2004): 63-87.

Hill, Dave. "Classical Marxism, Ideology and Education Policy." *Critical Education* 13, no. 1 (2022): 70-82.

Hood, Emily Jean and Tyson E. Lewis. "'Oohing and Ahhing': The Power of Thin(g)king in Art Education Research." *International Journal of Education Through Art* 17, no. 2 (2021): 223-233.

Jameson, Fredric. *Brecht and Method*. New York: Verso, 2000.

Jameson, Fredric. "Cognitive Mapping." In *Marxism and the In-*

terpretation of Culture. Ed. L. Grossberg and C. Nelson. Chicago: University of Illinois Press, 1988.

Jameson, Fredric. *Marxism and Form: Twentieth-Century Dialectical Theories of Literature*. Princeton: Princeton University Press, 1971.

Jameson, Fredric. "Postmodernism, or the Cultural Logic of Late Capitalism." *New Left Review* 1, no. 146 (1984): 53-92.

Katz, Mark. *Capturing Sound: How Technology has Changed Music*. Berkeley: University of California Press, 2010.

Kennedy, Stephen. *Future Sounds: The Temporality of Noise*. London: Bloomsbury, 2018.

Lefebvre, Henri. *Rhythmanalysis: Space, Time and Everyday Life*. Trans. S. Elden and G. Moore. London: Bloomsbury, 1992/2013.

Lefebvre, Henri. *The Production of Space*. Trans. D. Nicholson-Smith. Malden: Blackwell, 1974/1991.

Lefebvre, Henri. *The Urban Revolution*. Trans. R. Bononno. Minneapolis: University of Minnesota Press, 1970/2003.

Lefebvre, Henri. *Towards an Architecture of Enjoyment*. Trans. R. Bononno. Minneapolis: University of Minnesota Press, 2014.

Lefebvre, Henri. *Writings on Cities*. Trans. E. Kofman and E. Lebas. Malden: Blackwell, 1996.

Leininger, Noah. "Music, not Muddle: Re-Examining Soviet Sounds and the Socialist Project." *Liberation School*, 08 September 2020. Available here: liberationschool.org/re-examining-soviet-music-and-socialism.

Lewis, Tyson E. "A Marxist Education of the Encounter: Althusser, Interpellation, and the Seminar." *Rethinking Marxism* 29, no. 2 (2017): 303-317.

Lewis, Tyson E. *Inoperative Learning: A Radical Rewriting of Educational Potentialities*. New York: Routledge, 2018.

Lewis, Tyson E. "Studied Perception and a Phenomenology of Bodily Gesturality." In *Philosophy of Education 2013*. Ed. C. Mayo. Urbana: Philosophy of Education Society, 2013.

Lewis, Tyson E. *The Aesthetics of Education: Theatre, Curiosity, and Politics in the Work of Jacques Rancière and Paulo Freire*. London: Bloomsbury, 2012.

Lewis, Tyson E. "The Pedagogical Power of Things: Toward a Post-Intentional Phenomenology of Unlearning." *Cultural Critique* 98 (2018): 122-144.

Lewis, Tyson E. "Too Little, Too Late: Reflections on Fredric Jameson's Pedagogy of Form." *Rethinking Marxism* 21, no. 3 (2009): 438-452.

Liberation School Editorial Collective. "Introduction: Revolutionary Education and the Promotion of Socialist Consciousness." In *Revolutionary Education: Theory and Practice for Socialist Organizers*, 2nd ed. Ed. N. Brown. San Francisco: Liberation Media, 2022.

Lukács, Georg. *Lenin: A Study on the Unity of his Thought*. Trans. N. Jacobs. New York: Verso, 1924/2009.

Lynch, Kevin. *The Image of the City*. Cambridge: The MIT Press, 1960.

Malott, Curry S. "In Defense of Communism: Against Critical Pedagogy, Capitalism, and Trump." *Critical Education* 8, no. 1 (2017): 1-24.

Malott, Curry S. "Vindicating Stalin: Responding to Lefebvre." *Policy Futures in Education* 15, no. 4 (2017): 441-459.

Marasco, Robyn. "Althusser's Gramscian Debt: On Reading Out Loud." *Rethinking Marxism* 31, no. 3 (2019): 340-362.

Marx, Karl. *Capital: A Critique of Political Economy (Vol. 1): The Process of Capitalist Production*. Trans. S. Moore and E. Aveling. New York: International Publishers, 1867/1967.

Marx, Karl. *Capital: A Critique of Political Economy (Vol. 2): The Process of Circulation of Capital*. New York: International Publishers, 1885/1967.

Marx, Karl. *Capital: A Critique of Political Economy (Vol. 3): The Process of Capitalist Production as a Whole*. New York: International Publishers, 1894/1977.

Marx, Karl. *Economic and Philosophic Manuscripts of 1844*. Trans. M. Milligan. Mineola: Dover Publications, Inc., 1961/2007.

Marx, Karl. *Grundrisse: Foundations of the Critique of Political Economy (Rough Draft)*. Trans. M. Nicolaus. New York: Penguin Books, 1939/1973.

Marx, Karl. *The Eighteenth Brumaire of Louis Bonaparte*. Trans. C.P. Dutt. New York: International Publishers, 1852/1963.

Marx, Karl and Friedrich Engels. "Marx and Engels to August Bebel, Wilhelm Liebknecht, Wilhelm Bracke and Others (Circular Letter)." Trans. P. Ross and B. Ross. In *Marx and Engels Collected Works (Vol. 45): Letters 1874-79*. Ed. J.S. Allen, P.S. Foner, D.J. Struik, and W.W. Weinstone. London: Lawrence & Wisehart, 1879/2010.

Marx, Karl and Friedrich Engels. *The Communist Manifesto*. Trans. S. Moore. New York: Penguin, 1848/1967.

Marx, Karl and Frederick Engels. *The German Ideology: Part One*. Trans. C.J. Arthur. New York: International Publishers, 1932/1970.

McLaren, Peter. *Che Guevara, Paulo Freire, and the Pedagogy of Revolution*. Lanham: Rowman & Littlefield, 2000.

McLaren, Peter. "Revolutionary Critical Pedagogy." *Interactions* 6, no. 2 (2010): 1-11.

McLaren, Peter. *Schooling as Ritual Performance: Toward a Political Economy of Educational Symbols and Gestures*, 3rd ed. Lanham: Rowman & Littlefield, 1986/1999.

Merrifield, Andy. *The Politics of the Encounter: Urban Theory and Protest Under Planetary Urbanization*. Athens: The University of Georgia Press, 2013.

Mitchell, Don. "A Complicated Fetish." *Social & Cultural Geography* 15, no. 2 (2014): 125-126.

Mitchell, Don. *Mean Streets: Homelessness, Public Space, and the Limits of Capital*. Athens: The University of Georgia Press, 2020.

Montag, Warren. "Althusser's Authorless Theater." *differences* 26, no. 3 (2015): 43-53.

Moten, Fred. *In the Break: The Aesthetics of the Black Radical Tradition*. Minneapolis: University of Minnesota Press, 2003.

Mukařovský, Jan. *Aesthetic Function, Norm and Value as Social Facts*. Trans. M.E. Suino. Ann Arbor: University of Michigan Press, 1970.

Murawski, Michal. "Actually-Existing Success: Economics, Aesthetics, and the Specificity of (Still-)Socialist Urbanism." *Comparative Studies in Society and History* 60, no. 4 (2018): 907-937.

Nancy, Jean-Luc. *Listening*. Trans. C. Mandell. New York: Fordham University Press, 2007.

Pappachen, Megha Summer and Derek R. Ford. "Spreading Stupidity: Disability and Anti-Imperialist Resistance to Bio-Informational Capitalism." In *Bioinformational Philosophy and Postdigital Knowledge Ecologies*. Ed. M.A. Peters, P. Jandrić, and S. Hayes. New York: Springer, 2022.

Pickens, Therí Alyce. *Black Madness::Mad Blackness*. Durham: Duke University Press, 2019.

Ponce de León, Jennifer. *Another Aesthetics is Possible: Arts of Rebellion in the Fourth World War*. Durham: Duke University Press, 2021.

Ponce de León, Jennifer and Gabriel Rockhill. "Towards a Compositional Model of Ideology: Materialism, Aesthetics, and Cultural Revolution." *Philosophy Today* 64, no. 1 (2020): 95-116.

Rancière, Jacques. *Althusser's Lesson*. Trans. E. Battista. New York: Continuum, 1974/2011.

Rancière, Jacques. *The Flesh of Words: The Politics of Writing*. Trans. C. Mandell. Stanford: Stanford University Press, 1998/2004.

Rich, Stephen G. "Some Unnoticed Aspects of the School Use of Phonographs." *Journal of Educational Method* 3, no. 1 (1923): 108-114.

Rikowski, Glenn. "Crisis." In *Critical Reflections on the Language of Neoliberalism in Education: Dangerous Words and Discourses of Possibility*. Ed. S. Themelis. New York: Routledge, 2021.

Ritchey, Marianna. *Composing Capital: Classical Music in the Neoliberal Era*. Chicago: The University of Chicago Press, 2019.

Ritchey, Marianna. "Resisting Usefulness: Music and the Political Imagination." *Current Musicology* 108 (2021): 26-52.

Robinson, Cedric. *Black Marxism: The Making of the Black Radical Tradition*. Chapel Hill: The University of North Carolina Press, 1983/2000.

Robinson, Dylan. *Hungry Listening: Resonant Theory for Indig-*

enous Sound Studies. Minneapolis: University of Minnesota Press, 2020.

Rockhill, Gabriel. *Radical History and the Politics of Art*. New York: Columbia University Press, 2014.

Rockhill, Gabriel. "Temporal Economies and the Prison of the Present: From the Crisis of the Now to Liberation Time." *Diacritics* 47, no. 1 (2019): 16-29.

Rockhill, Gabriel. "The CIA & the Frankfurt School's Anti-Communism." *The Philosophical Salon*, 27 June 2022. Available here: thephilosophicalsalon.com/the-cia-the-frankfurt-schools-anti-communism.

Schweik, Susan M. *The Ugly Laws: Disability in Public*. New York: New York University Press, 2009.

Spivak, Gayatri Chakravorty. *A Critique of Postcolonial Reason: Toward a History of the Vanishing Present*. Cambridge: Harvard University Press, 1999.

Stanek, Łukasz. *Henri Lefebvre on Space: Architecture, Urban Research, and the Production of Theory*. Minneapolis: University of Minnesota Press, 2011.

Szymanski, Albert. *Is the Red Flag Flying? The Political Economy of the Soviet Union*. London: Zed Books, 1979.

Taylor, Timothy D. *Music and Capitalism: A History of the Present*. Chicago: The University of Chicago Press, 2017.

Walker, Gavin. *The Sublime Perversion of Capital: Marxist Theory and the Politics of History in Modern Japan*. Durham: Duke University Press, 2016.

Wozniak, Jason. "Creating the Conditions for Free Time in the Debt Economy: On Stealing Time in and Through Education." *Philosophical Inquiry in Education* 29, no. 2 (2022): 117-131.

Wozniak, Jason. "Towards a Rhythmanalysis of Debt Dressage: Education as Rhythmic Resistance in Everyday Indebted Life." *Policy Futures in Education* 15, no. 4 (2017): 495-508.

Zarecor, Kimberly Elman. "What was so Socialist about the Socialist City? Second World Urbanity in Europe." *Journal of Urban History* 44, no. 1 (2018): 95-117.

INDEX

V

Value 7, 31, 33, 142

W

Wozniak, Jason 23, 102, 109, 111, 133, 144, 145

Printed in the USA
CPSIA information can be obtained
at www.ICGtesting.com
LVHW071318011023
759824LV00004B/24